S320

INFECTIOUS DISEASE

Library

6

MODELLING EPIDEMICS

prepared for the Course Team by
Paddy Farrington

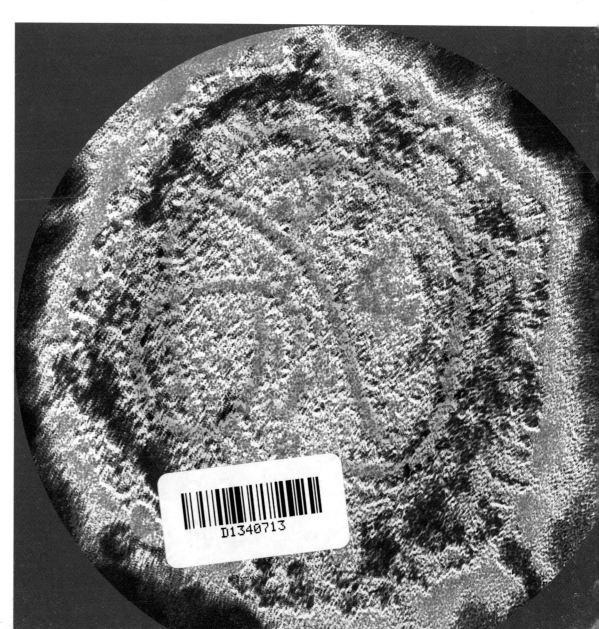

Cover picture: Coloured transmission electron micrograph of a section through mumps virus in a capsule. The long, thin chains (red) contain RNA genetic material enclosed within the capsule (pink).

This publication forms part of an Open University course S320 *Infectious Disease*. The complete list of texts which make up this course can be found at the back. Details of this and other Open University courses can be obtained from the Course Information and Advice Centre, PO Box 724, The Open University, Milton Keynes MK7 6ZS, United Kingdom: tel. +44 (0)1908 653231, e-mail general-enquiries@open.ac.uk

Alternatively, you may visit the Open University website at http://www.open.ac.uk where you can learn more about the wide range of courses and packs offered at all levels by The Open University.

To purchase a selection of Open University course materials visit the webshop at www.ouw.co.uk, or contact Open University Worldwide, Michael Young Building, Walton Hall, Milton Keynes MK7 6AA, United Kingdom for a brochure. tel. +44 (0)1908 858785; fax +44 (0)1908 858787; e-mail ouwenq@open.ac.uk

The Open University
Walton Hall, Milton Keynes
MK7 6AA

First published 2003.

Edited, designed and typeset by The Open University.

Printed and bound in the United Kingdom by the Alden Group, Oxford.

ISBN 0 7492 56605

1.1

THE S320 COURSE TEAM

Course Team Chair

Michael Gillman

Course Manager

Viki Burnage

Course Team Assistant

Dawn Partner

Course Team Authors

Basiro Davey (Books 1 & 7)

Tim Halliday (Book 5)

Paddy Farrington (Book 6)

Michael Gillman (Books 1 & 5)

Hilary MacQueen (Books 2 & 4)

David Male (Books 1, 3 & 7)

Consultant Authors

Eric Bowers (Book 2)

Christine Heading (Book 7)

Laura Hibberts (Books 2 & 4)

Ralph Muller (Book 7)

Editors

Pat Forster

Gilly Riley

Margaret Swithenby

Academic Reader

Mary Manley

External Course Assessor

Bo Drasar

OU Graphic Design

Roger Courthold

Sian Lewis

Video Editing

Wilf Eynon

Michael Francis

CD-ROM Production

Greg Black

Phil Butcher

BBC Production

Martin Kemp

Rights Executive

Christine Brady

Picture Research

Lydia Eaton

Indexer

Jean Macqueen

Course Websites

Patrina Law

Louise Olney

Sue Dugher

CONTENTS

CONCEPTS AND DATA

You will not need access to a computer to study any of Book 6, though occasionally cross-references are made to case study materials on CD-ROMs; these could be consulted at a later stage if you wish.

At several points in each chapter you might find it useful to use a calculator, both to follow the calculations in the text and to do the short illustrative exercises. You will only require the simple arithmetic functions (addition, subtraction, multiplication and division); an optional exercise also involves taking square roots.

Book 6 also makes some use of mathematical notation. The skills required to make sense of this are an ability to interpret symbolic notation (for example, an infection rate might be represented by the Greek symbol λ, (lambda), and to manipulate simple mathematical equations, mainly in the form of ratios. For example, if $a = b/c$, then it follows that $c = b/a$. Guidance on how to handle and interpret such equations is given where appropriate.

1.1 Introduction

All human diseases involve, to a greater or lesser extent, interactions between ourselves and our physical and social environments. For example, some cancers are caused by environmental exposures to sunlight, chemicals or radioactivity; smoking causes lung cancer; heart disease is related to diet.

Infectious diseases are no exception: our social and physical environment, and the ways in which we shape them, have a direct bearing on the spread of infections, and indeed on the emergence of new infections. For example, in the 1980s and 90s, contamination of the UK egg supply with *Salmonella enteritidis* led to an increase in the incidence of salmonellosis. The consumption of meat products infected with BSE led to the emergence of a new variant of Creutzfeldt Jakob Disease. War and conflict invariably result in increased infection rates among civilian populations, for example in the crowded and often insanitary conditions of refugee camps. Lack of access to clean water favours the transmission of water-borne infections like cholera and other diarrhoeal diseases. Tuberculosis can thrive in conditions of overcrowding and has sometimes been called a disease of poverty.

For infectious diseases as for other types of diseases, genetic, social and environmental factors have a substantial impact on susceptibility to infection, and on the clinical course of the disease. For example, nutritional status influences the clinical course of many infectious diseases of childhood. This goes some way towards explaining the huge disparity in mortality attributable to infectious diseases between developing and developed countries. Such effects are sometimes called **risk factors**, in that they influence outcomes without necessarily being their sole cause.

However, social factors play a uniquely fundamental role for infectious diseases, in that they also determine the transmission of infectious agents. Thus they operate at the level of *mechanisms*, as well as risk factors. The key concept is that of contact, however defined: without contacts between hosts of some sort, infectious diseases do not spread.

For this reason, no microbiological, medical or indeed risk-based epidemiological account of infectious diseases can be deemed in any way complete. To understand infectious diseases it is necessary to understand the processes that enable the transmission of infection to proceed. As it turns out, a few simple concepts and models go a long way towards explaining how many different infections spread and become established, and hence can help guide strategies for their control and ultimate eradication.

Epidemiology is the study of the health of populations. It draws upon knowledge from the fields of anthropology, biology, medicine, sociology and statistics. Its central paradigm is that health and disease have social dimensions, knowledge of which can illuminate the causes and hence inform the prevention of ill-health in individuals.

It is not possible to give a complete account of the epidemiology of infectious diseases here: this is subject matter enough for an entire course. The epidemiology of measles, for example, is totally different from that of HIV. Indeed, the epidemiology of measles in Western Europe is totally different from that in sub-Saharan Africa, and the same applies to HIV. However the principles governing the transmission of infectious agents can be treated in a common, and relatively simple, framework, at least with the aid of some simplifying assumptions.

Book 6 is about these concepts and models. Chapter 1 is a short introduction to the key concepts of risks and rates and to data sources. Also in this chapter we introduce perhaps the most important concept of all in infectious disease epidemiology, namely the *basic reproduction number*, or R_0. Chapter 2 describes a modelling framework for infectious diseases, the so-called SIR model, and explores the fundamental notion of contact. In Chapter 3 we shall move on to the problem of estimating R_0, contact rates and other parameters for endemic infections, using another key parameter, the *herd immunity level*. Chapter 4 applies these methods to investigate the population level impact of immunisation, providing some quantitative guidance for vaccination strategies. Finally, in Chapter 5, which is much shorter than the previous chapters, we shall investigate the phenomenon of *epidemicity*.

1.2 Risks and rates

Because epidemiology deals with the health of populations rather than individuals, its methods are statistical. No knowledge of these techniques is required here, other than an acquaintance with the notions of **risk** and **rate**.

If the risk is zero, then the event will never happen. If the risk is 1, it will always happen.

In epidemiology, a risk is a probability, that is, a number between 0 and 1, indicating the chance of an event happening. One might think, for example, of the risk of becoming infected with rubella virus during pregnancy. Risks are estimated using proportions. For example, imagine that out of 1000 pregnant women, two are infected by rubella virus. Then an estimate of the risk of rubella virus infection during pregnancy would be

$$\frac{2}{1000} = 0.002$$

Note that in this calculation we have assumed nothing about how many of the 1000 women actually came into contact with rubella virus.

A common use of risks in epidemiology is in computing probabilities of an outcome event, which could be disease, infection or death, given exposure to one or more potential risk factors. Thus, in that context,

$$\text{risk} = \frac{\text{number of persons experiencing the event}}{\text{number of persons exposed to the potential risk factor}}$$

A **risk factor** is a variable associated with an increased risk of disease or infection. For instance, to continue the previous example, having young children might be regarded as a risk factor for rubella in pregnancy, since young children are at high risk of contracting rubella virus which they might then pass on to their pregnant mother. Much of epidemiology is concerned with identifying risk factors for disease.

○ Age is a risk factor for measles. Can you explain why, and identify the age groups most at risk?

● Adults are more likely than children to have developed immunity to measles during previous exposure to the virus. So adults are at lower risk of measles than children.

Risk factors vary between infectious diseases. For example, age is a risk factor for both measles and shingles. However, unlike measles, older people are at higher risk of shingles than children. This is because shingles is caused by the reactivation of varicella zoster virus acquired earlier in life when it produces the disease known as chickenpox. Reactivation results from a decline in immunity levels, and hence occurs more frequently in older people.

Note that risk factors are not necessarily *causal*: being young cannot in any sense be said to cause measles infection, for example. However, some non-causal risk factors can influence outcomes. Identifying such risk factors can help to suggest intervention strategies. For example, in many developing countries, malnutrition and low level of maternal education are risk factors for infant and children's deaths, many of which are due to infectious diseases. Improving educational opportunities for young mothers and ensuring an equitable distribution of food are thus effective public health interventions to reduce infant and child mortality.

Though it is as well to reflect on the cultural specificity of what might validly be regarded as a 'cause'. Lack of awareness of the cultural context can reduce the effectiveness of prevention strategies, for example against malaria in some parts of Africa.

Risk factors are evaluated by comparing the risk in individuals exposed to the risk factor with the risk in individuals not exposed to the risk factor. A typical use of this approach is in investigating outbreaks.

○ An outbreak of salmonellosis has occurred among guests who have all attended a wedding reception. Investigations show that, of 84 guests who report having eaten chicken, 21 were ill, compared to 3 out of the 40 guests who did not eat chicken. Calculate the infection risks in those who ate, and those who did not eat chicken. What might you conclude? What further investigations might you undertake?

● The risk in those who ate chicken is 21/84 = 0.25, compared to 3/40 = 0.075 in those who did not. So the risk is over three times higher in those who ate chicken. This might suggest (but does not prove) that contaminated chicken

Serotypes are types of one organism classified according to their antigenic properties.

was the cause of the outbreak. Laboratory tests could help confirm this hypothesis, for example if the same salmonella serotype was identified in the chicken and the infected guests. (You will learn more about how causative agents in food-poisoning outbreaks are identified in Book 7, Chapter 3.)

In the case of very many infections, such as those caused by measles virus, *Bordetella pertussis*, rotavirus, and hepatitis A virus, becoming infected at some point in life is a near certainty, unless an appropriate vaccination programme has been implemented. Thus the lifetime risk of acquiring varicella zoster infection is close to 1. But this tells us nothing about when the infection is likely to occur. For this we need a different measure, called a **rate**.

A rate is a measure of occurrence per unit time. The key difference between a rate and a probability is the 'per unit time'. For example, the lifetime risk of dying is 1 for all of us. But in developed countries such as the UK, the mortality rate (or, more precisely, the age-specific mortality rate, calculated for each year of age) is quite low until people reach their seventies, when it rises steeply.

A rate is estimated as follows:

$$\text{rate} = \frac{\text{number of events}}{\text{number of persons exposed} \times \text{average duration of exposure}}$$

For example, suppose that over the course of 12 months, 20 colds occur within an office of 100 staff. What is the monthly rate at which colds occur? The relevant exposure here is 'working in the office', so 100 persons are exposed, each for 12 months. The monthly rate is

$$\frac{20}{100 \times 12} \approx 0.017$$

We have used the symbol $\approx$ ('approximately equal to') here rather than $=$ ('equal to') to indicate that we have rounded the answer. Note that, unlike risks, rates have *units*; in this case the rate is per month. Also, it is quite possible that some people had more than one cold during the 12 months: the numerator here is events, not persons experiencing an event.

In a fraction written as a/b, a is called the numerator and b the denominator.

The rate at which *new* instances of a disease occur in a population is called the **incidence rate**, or just incidence. Thus we would say that, in the office population above, the incidence of common colds was 0.017 per month.

○ Suppose that among the 350 children attending a primary school, over a period of four weeks, 38 are absent due to measles. Calculate the incidence per week of measles in this population.

● The incidence is $\dfrac{38}{350 \times 4} \approx 0.027$

The proportion of the population with a particular infection at a given time is called the **prevalence** of infection. For acute infections, which resolve over a short period of days or weeks, there are generally few current cases at any one time (compared to the size of the population), and so measures of incidence are more commonly used than measures of prevalence. However, for infections lasting much longer, such as HIV infection, or those with a carrier state such as infection with hepatitis

B virus, both incidence and prevalence measures are used. In Book 6, however, we use primarily incidence rates.

Estimating risks and rates is perhaps the easiest aspect of epidemiology. The real challenge lies in interpreting them correctly; it is all too easy to jump to conclusions and declare that a risk factor 'causes' the disease, when in fact other, non-causal explanations exist. That two events are *associated* does not imply that one causes the other. For example, the AIDS epidemic in the USA, the UK and some other Western countries began in male gay populations, which led some to conclude that AIDS was caused by sex between men. In fact there is no such causal link, and in most parts of the world AIDS is predominantly transmitted by heterosexual sex.

Finally, it is worth pointing out that, in the scientific literature (including the epidemiological literature), the distinction between *risks* (probabilities of occurrence) and *rates* (numbers of occurrences per unit time) is blurred. This is partly due to an incoherent terminology: some risks are commonly called rates. For example, the infant mortality 'rate' is in fact the risk (usually expressed per 1000 live births) that a child will die within the first 12 months of life. Another important example is the **attack rate** of an infection: this is just the risk of infection in a defined group. Generally, such terminological inconsistencies matter little. In Book 6 we shall point out when they arise, but shall otherwise follow common usage.

1.3 The basic reproduction number

In addition to risks and rates, you will need to know some other concepts, the most important of which is the **basic reproduction number** of an infection, denoted R_0. Because of its central role in infectious disease epidemiology, we introduce it here. (Recall that the scene was set for discussion of R_0 in Book 5, Chapter 3, with respect to the spread of malaria.)

R_0 is pronounced 'are-nought'.

Imagine a population that is totally susceptible for a given infection, that is, one in which nobody is immune to the infection. Into this population, introduce a single typical infectious individual known as an **infective**. That individual will make contacts with others and hence will transmit the infection to some number of other persons during the period in which he or she is infectious; these are called *secondary* infections. The basic reproduction number of the infection is the average number of secondary infections. The definition is represented in Figure 1.1.

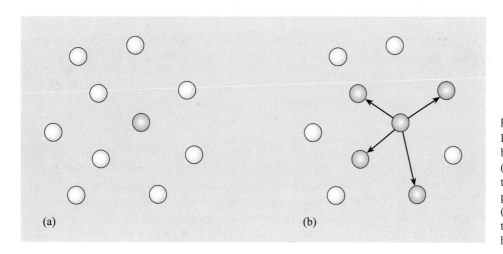

(a)   (b)

FIGURE 1.1
Diagrammatic representation of the basic reproduction number R_0.
(a) A single infective (represented by the purple dot) is introduced into a population of susceptibles (yellow dots).
(b) This initial infective transmits the infection to R_0 others on average; here $R_0 = 4$.

The basic reproduction number is neither a risk nor a rate: it is just a number. It can take any positive value (or zero). Note the rather theoretical character of its definition: in the case of measles, for instance, there is probably no population on Earth that is totally susceptible. Yet, as it turns out, and as you will see later in Book 6, it is possible to estimate R_0 for measles, and for other infectious agents.

For uncommon infections, on the other hand, R_0 may sometimes be calculated directly.

○ For example, suppose that, in an outbreak of Marburg fever (a viral haemorrhagic fever) in a large susceptible community, a total of 6 people were directly infected by the first case, before control measures were introduced. In a second outbreak of Marburg fever in a different but similar community, a total of 9 people were infected by the first case. Obtain an estimate of R_0.

● R_0 is the average number directly infected by one case in a susceptible population. In the first outbreak, 6 people were infected by 1 initial case. In the second outbreak, 9 people were infected by 1 initial case. So, overall, $6 + 9 = 15$ people were infected by 2 initial cases. So the average number directly infected per initial case is $(6 + 9)/2 = 7.5$. Thus an estimate of R_0 is 7.5. This is only a rough estimate, since it is based on only two outbreaks.

R_0 is important because it encapsulates the relationship between an infection and its physical and social environment. The number of secondary infections depends on the ability of the infectious organism to survive outside the host and to migrate from one host to the next, which in turn depends on biological and environmental factors. It depends on the infection-host interaction through, for instance, the duration of the infectious period. It also depends on the frequency and type of contacts that take place within the population, which vary according to the environmental, social and cultural context (see Box 1.1).

Box 1.1   HIV and kuru: examples of social and cultural factors in the transmission of infectious diseases

Learning about 'local' sexual practices was important in developing prevention strategies against HIV all over the world, and in predicting the future course of the HIV epidemic. Until the 1980s, little reliable information was available in the UK about sexual practices, frequency of sexual contacts or partner change, and risk reduction practices such as condom use. Several large-scale surveys of sexual practices and attitudes have since been conducted in the UK, the first being the National Survey of Sexual Attitudes and Lifestyles (NATSSAL). Difficult issues of confidentiality and survey design had to be resolved before the surveys could go ahead.

Kuru, a fatal neurodegenerative disease, was prevalent among the South Fore people of New Guinea until the last century, particularly though not exclusively among women. Early theories that the disease was genetic in origin were discounted due to its high mortality. In the 1960s, Gadjusek and colleagues showed that kuru was infectious, transmitted by contact with and consumption of human tissue of deceased relatives occurring during mortuary cannibalistic rites. The higher prevalence of disease in women was due to their greater contact with infectious material during these rites. Kuru is related to Creutzfeldt Jakob disease (CJD) and other transmissible spongiform encephalopathies (TSEs). Originally it was assumed that the infectious agents in TSEs were viruses. In the 1980s, it was suggested that a new kind of infectious agent, a prion, was responsible. Prions are proteins, and contain no nucleic acid genome. The discovery that proteins alone can transmit infectious diseases came as a considerable surprise to the scientific community; see Book 2 for a full discussion.

As you will see later in Book 6, R_0 plays a central role in infectious disease epidemiology. One reason is that if R_0 is less than (or equal to) one, then the infection will die out, whereas if R_0 is greater than one, then there may be a large epidemic and the infection may become *endemic*, that is, ever-present.

To understand this, it is useful to think in terms of **generations** of infected individuals. An outbreak begins with one or more introductory cases. These form generation zero. The introductory cases may directly infect other people, who form the first generation of spread. These in turn infect a second generation of cases, and so on. For example, Figure 1.2 shows the dates of onset of symptoms in cases of measles during a school outbreak in the USA. The outbreak is thought to have originated from a visitor to the school, who infected two children in the first generation of spread. During the early stages of the outbreak, the cases are clumped together in generations about 10–14 days apart (later on the generations begin to overlap and become more difficult to distinguish).

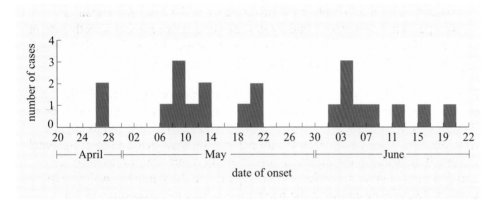

FIGURE 1.2
Measles onset dates in a school outbreak, 1985, in Corpus Christi, Texas, USA.

The outbreak depicted in Figure 1.2 occurred in an immunised population, and so petered out after a few generations. Consider what would happen in a large, totally susceptible population. One infection causes, on average, R_0 secondary infections, which constitutes the first generation of cases. Each one of these will also cause, on average, R_0 infections, so that there will be, on average, $R_0 \times R_0 = R_0^2$ (i.e. R_0 squared) infections at the second generation. At the third generation there will be, on average, $R_0 \times R_0 \times R_0 = R_0^3$ (i.e. R_0 cubed) infections, and so on. The average number of infections in successive generations will begin to increase very quickly if $R_0 > 1$ (i.e. R_0 greater than 1), and reduce to zero if $R_0 < 1$ (i.e. R_0 less than 1), as illustrated in Figure 1.3. (It will also go to zero if $R_0 = 1$, due to chance fluctuations.)

○ Suppose that $R_0 = 3$. Calculate the number of infections, on average, in successive generations, following the introduction of a single infection. Can this trend continue indefinitely?

● The average numbers in successive generations are 1, 3, 9, 27, 81, 243, 729.... The trend cannot continue indefinitely, as eventually the number of susceptibles will be depleted thereby limiting the spread of infection. But by then a large epidemic will have occurred.

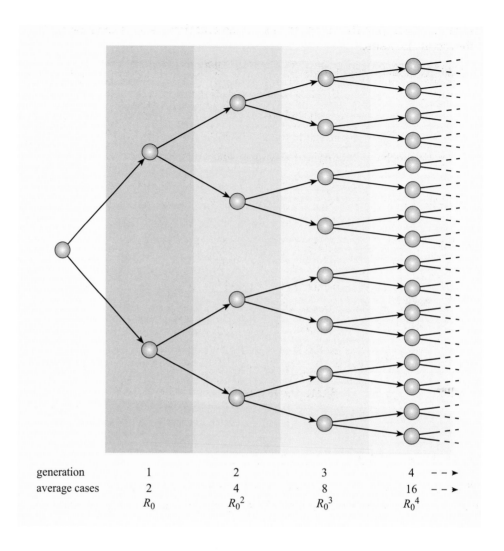

generation	1	2	3	4	– – ➤
average cases	2	4	8	16	– – ➤
	R_0	R_0^2	R_0^3	R_0^4	

FIGURE 1.3

The spread of an infection when $R_0 = 2$.

A second reason why R_0 is important is that the larger its value, the more effort is needed to control the infection. This makes sense intuitively: the larger the value of R_0, the steeper the growth of the epidemic, and hence the more difficult it is to control it. We shall refine this idea in Chapter 4.

○ Table 1.1 shows some typical values of R_0 for selected infections. Which infection is likely to require most effort to control? Which is likely to prove easiest to control? Is the magnitude of R_0 the only relevant factor in controlling an infection?

● Measles and whooping cough both have the greatest R_0 value ranges of 13–18 and so are the most difficult to control of the infections listed. Note that the infection with the lowest value of R_0 in Table 1.1 is smallpox, which has been eradicated globally. The magnitude of R_0 is not the only factor which determines how difficult it is to control an infection. Other relevant factors include, for example, the availability of effective vaccines, and the existence of a health care network to carry out large-scale vaccination programmes.

The terms *eliminate* and *eradicate* have specific meanings that will be made precise in Chapter 4.

Table 1.1 Values of R_0 in different locations and time periods for selected infectious diseases.

Infectious disease	Location and time period	R_0
measles	England & Wales, 1947–50	13–14
	Ghana, 1960–68	14–15
	Eastern Nigeria, 1960–68	16–17
whooping cough	England & Wales, 1944–78	16–18
	USA, 1943	16–17
chickenpox	England & Wales, 1944–68	10–12
	USA, 1943	10–11
mumps	England & Wales, 1960–80	11–14
	Netherlands, 1970–80	11–14
rubella	England & Wales, 1960–70	6–7
	Poland, 1970–77	11–12
	Gambia, 1976	15–16
polio	Netherlands, 1960	6–7
HIV	Uganda, 1985–87	10–11
smallpox	West Africa, 1968–73	3–5

1.4 Infectious disease data

The three main sources of epidemiological data on infectious diseases we shall discuss in Book 6 are case reports, laboratory reports, and serological surveys.

Case reports

Case reports are counts of disease, usually diagnosed by medical examination on the basis of signs and symptoms, and notified through passive or active surveillance systems. A **passive surveillance system** is one that relies entirely on the initiative of the individual making the report, usually a physician or public health official. In an **active surveillance system**, on the other hand, cases are *sought*, for example by means of questionnaires. Some surveillance systems do not aim to capture all events, but instead seek comprehensive reporting from a limited number of committed participants, for example GPs or paediatricians; these are called **sentinel surveillance systems**. Data from sentinel systems are often converted into population rates rather than raw counts, since the numbers of participants in the scheme may vary over time.

A prerequisite for most surveillance systems is the existence of a robust public health infrastructure. This exists in many, but not all developed countries. Some developing countries, for example Cuba, also have good quality surveillance systems. In many developing countries, however, the infrastructure required for systematic collection of disease surveillance data is not available.

The statutory notification system for infectious diseases in the UK is a passive reporting system (see Box 1.2). The USA also uses a national reporting system, coordinated by the Centers for Disease Control and Prevention (CDC). France has a sentinel reporting system, the Réseau Sentinelles, based on a subset of general practitioners. The Royal College of General Practitioners (RCGP) in the UK also runs a sentinel surveillance system (you saw examples of data from this source in Book 1, Chapter 1). The British Paediatric Association has an active surveillance programme for selected, generally rare, paediatric infections.

Box 1.2   The UK statutory notification system

The statutory requirement for the notification of certain infectious diseases came into being towards the end of the 19th century. Diseases such as cholera, diphtheria, smallpox and typhoid had to be reported in London from 1891 and in the rest of England and Wales from 1899. The list of diseases increased over the decades and now stands at about 30. Originally, the head of the family or landlord had the responsibility of reporting the disease to the 'proper officer' of the local authority. Now this is restricted to the attending medical practitioner, either in the patient's home or at a surgery or hospital.

The prime purpose of the notification system is *speed* in detecting possible outbreaks and epidemics. Accuracy of diagnosis is secondary and since 1968, clinical suspicion of a notifiable infection is all that is required. Originally, statistics were collected nationally at the Registrar General's Office, who already collected data on births, marriages and deaths. The Office was later known as the Office of Population Censuses and Surveys (OPCS) and now as the Office for National Statistics (ONS), but in 1997 the responsibility for administering the notification system was transferred to the Communicable Disease Surveillance Centre (CDSC). The proper officers, who are usually consultants in communicable disease control (CCDCs), are required every week to inform CDSC of details of each case of each disease that has been notified. CDSC has responsibility for collating these weekly returns and publishing analyses of local and national trends.

Figure 1.4 shows graphs over time of several notifiable diseases in the UK. The interpretation of case reports requires some care. For example, apparent changes in incidence could be due to changes in reporting practice or heightened awareness. Nevertheless, case reports (or rates derived from sentinel reporting schemes) are a valuable tool in identifying trends and other patterns.

○ The general trend in infectious diseases in the UK during the 20th century was downwards, at least before the HIV epidemic started. Figure 1.4 confirms that this is broadly true for diphtheria, typhoid, measles, scarlet fever, and whooping cough. However, for polio the graph tells a very different story: there was a big increase in the decade after 1945, which was stemmed by the introduction of mass vaccination. What are the possible reasons for this increase?

● In interpreting time trends it is important to consider effects due to (a) demographic changes (a larger population would produce more cases, even if the infection rate remained constant); (b) changes in the reporting system or in reporting practices (for example, the true or perceived severity of a disease will affect the likelihood of it being reported); (c) changes in the clinical

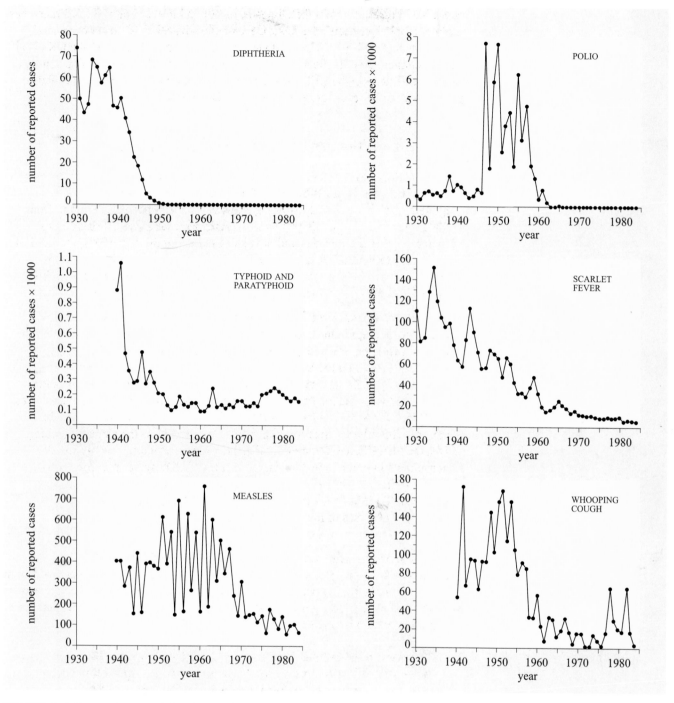

FIGURE 1.4 Reports by year of diphtheria, typhoid and paratyphoid, measles, polio, scarlet fever, and whooping cough in the UK, 1930–1985.

manifestation of the infection. In the case of polio, (a) is insufficient to explain the large variation in reports. The truth is probably a combination of (b) and (c): polio became a major public health issue in the post-war period, as the incidence of acute flaccid paralysis increased (though probably not the incidence of polio virus infection). The reasons for this change will be touched upon later in Book 6.

Flaccid paralysis is a form of muscle paralysis caused by destruction of the nerve tissue by the polio virus (see the polio case study associated with Book 7).

A further problem with case reports based on purely clinical criteria is their lack of specificity, which means that many cases attributed to an infection may in fact be due to other causes. This is particularly problematic for some rare infections. Thus, for example, since the introduction of the combined measles, mumps and rubella (MMR) vaccine in the UK in 1988, reports of measles have fallen. However, as already mentioned in Book 1, Chapter 1, most of the reported measles cases are not measles at all, but are caused by other infections that produce a rash, such as parvovirus infection. Thus case reports of measles are currently unreliable for studying the epidemiology of measles in the UK.

☐ On the other hand, measles case reports prior to mass vaccination were very useful indeed. Can you suggest why?

⬤ Prior to the introduction of mass vaccination, the incidence of measles was very high. Most of the reported rash-like illness was indeed measles; other infections accounted for only a small proportion of the total cases.

Laboratory reports

In order to circumvent the problem of non-specific reports, it is necessary to use laboratory-based identification techniques, such as culture, typing or serological testing (as described in Book 4). **Laboratory reports** are a second major source of infectious disease data. These are counts of infections, which have been confirmed by laboratory identification. Laboratory reports suffer similar problems of potential bias as case reports, since most often clinical diagnosis precedes laboratory confirmation, and hence changes in clinical awareness will also affect laboratory reports. Also, confirmation might only be sought in serious cases, and hence laboratory reports might be *less representative* than case reports. However, they are undoubtedly *more specific* than case reports. The major sources of laboratory-based infectious disease data in the UK are the Public Health Laboratory Service (PHLS), which collects laboratory reports from laboratories in England and Wales, and the Scottish Centre for Infection and Environmental Health (SCIEH) in Scotland. After 2003, the PHLS was incorporated into the Health Protection Agency (HPA). Figure 1.5 shows laboratory reports for selected infections.

☐ The infections graphed in Figure 1.5 have the following characteristics. (a) Rotavirus is a viral enteric infection, accounting for much paediatric diarrhoea; (b) *Clostridium difficile* is associated with antibiotic use, and is of particular concern in hospitals; (c) *Salmonella derby* and (f) a strain of *Salmonella typhimurium* known as DT104, and (d) *Shigella sonnei* (a cause of dysentry), are all bacterial enteric infections; (e) influenza B is a respiratory infection. For each infection, comment on (i) the overall trend in reports, and (ii) any epidemics or cyclical effects.

⬤ (i) *C. difficile* and *S. typhimurium* DT104 both show increasing trends. It is not clear from these data alone whether the trend is genuine, or due to improved reporting. (ii) Rotavirus and *S. typhimurium* DT104 have marked annual cycles, peaking in winter/spring for rotavirus and summer for *S. typhimurium*. Influenza B has irregular epidemics. There appears to have been an epidemic of *S. sonnei* in 1991–93. In spite of the small numbers, it looks like *S. derby* has autumn epidemic peaks. There are no obvious epidemic fluctuations for *C. difficile*.

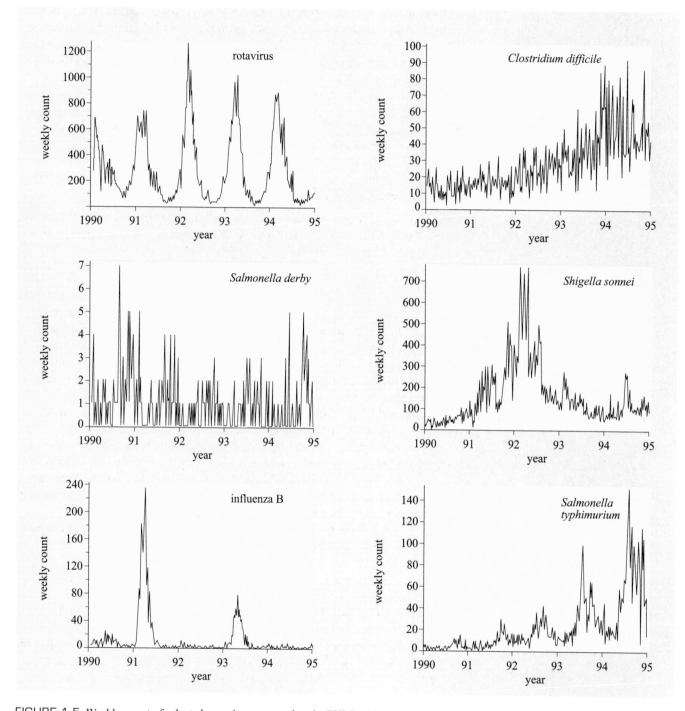

FIGURE 1.5 Weekly count of selected organisms reported to the PHLS, 1990–95. (a) rotavirus, (b) *Clostridium difficile*, (c) *Salmonella derby*, (d) *Shigella sonnei*, (e) influenza B, (f) *Salmonella typhimurium* DT104.

However, both case reports and laboratory reports suffer from a major shortcoming, at least for the purposes of studying the dynamics of transmission — lack of completeness. In other words, only a fraction of cases are reported or tested in the laboratory. As a result, many infections are never documented. For example, studies of notified cases of whooping cough in the UK suggest that fewer than 20% of cases are notified. On the other hand, lack of completeness need not be a hindrance to the study of trends, provided that the *proportions* of cases reported remain constant over time.

A further difficulty stems from the fact that not all infections result in disease states sufficiently serious to warrant seeking medical advice. For example, only about 60% of mumps infections produce clinical symptoms. The remaining 40%, which are called **sub-clinical infections**, will never come to the attention of the general practitioner, and so will never be notified or sampled for laboratory analysis. Nevertheless, individuals with sub-clinical infections can pass on the pathogen, and so play an important role in the transmission of the infection. For example, fewer than 10% of polio virus infections are symptomatic (and fewer than 1% cause paralysis), but asymptomatic infected individuals can transmit polio virus.

Serological surveys

Data from surveys of population immunity provide one way of circumventing such difficulties. In such a survey, individuals are tested to establish their immune status. Provided that the survey is representative, it can provide a profile of population immunity, which is not biased by non-ascertainment of sub-clinical infections (though it does rely on the accuracy of the test). Perhaps one of the oldest such techniques is the intra-dermal tuberculin sensitivity test for tuberculosis (the Heaf test is described in the *Tuberculosis* CD-ROM). Today, the most commonly used surveys are **serological surveys**, usually tested using ELISA (*enzyme-linked immunosorbent assay*; see Book 4). Data from a survey of antibodies against the mumps virus in the UK prior to the introduction of MMR vaccine are shown in Figure 1.6. It should be mentioned however that for some infectious agents, such as *Bordetella pertussis*, the bacterial cause of whooping cough, there is as yet no agreed serological correlate of immunity. In this case, population surveys of antibody prevalence are difficult to interpret in terms of population immunity.

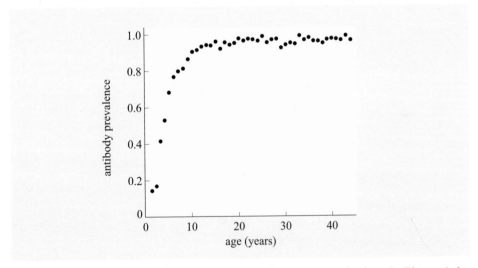

FIGURE 1.6
Proportion of the population with IgG antibody to mumps by age, UK, 1986–87.

For mumps, presence of IgG antibodies indicates past infection. In Figure 1.6, the proportion of individuals with IgG antibody to mumps increases with age until about 15 years of age, then reaches a plateau. Can you explain why?

The duration of exposure to infection increases with age. Hence the risk of past infection increases with age. Correspondingly, the proportion of individuals with antibodies to mumps increases with age. After about 15 years of age, virtually everyone in this population has been exposed to the mumps virus, so the curve reaches a plateau close to 100%.

Finally, it is important to mention data on vaccine coverage. Good data are unavailable in many countries, in both the developed and developing worlds. In England and Wales, vaccine coverage data are collected quarterly by the Communicable Disease Surveillance Centre (see the *Resources* section of the course website).

Summary of Chapter 1

1   The subject of epidemiology is the study of health in populations. An important aspect of the epidemiology of infectious diseases is the study of how infections are transmitted within populations.

2   Basic measures of epidemiology include risks and rates. A risk is the probability that an event, such as infection or disease, occurs within a defined group. A rate is the number of occurrences per unit time in a given population.

3   An important measure in infectious disease epidemiology is the basic reproduction number, R_0. This is the average number of individuals directly infected by a single infective introduced into a population that is completely susceptible to the infection.

4   If R_0 is less than or equal to 1, the infection will die out in the population. If R_0 is greater than 1, the infection may become endemic. The larger the value of R_0, the more difficult the infection is to control.

5   Commonly used epidemiological data for infectious diseases include case reports, laboratory reports, and serological survey data. Awareness of the possible shortcomings of these data, for example because of lack of completeness, or diagnostic inaccuracy, is required when interpreting them.

2 MODELLING INFECTIOUS DISEASES

In this chapter we develop a simple modelling framework for the transmission of infections. We consider only pathogenic microbes transmitted directly from person to person. Thus, for example, we shall not consider infectious agents for which the presence of an animal reservoir plays a major role, like toxoplasma or many salmonellas, or vector-borne infections like malaria or yellow fever in which the pathogen is indirectly transmitted between humans. Nor shall we consider the multicellular parasites, such as helminths. The reason for restricting the scope of the models in this way is to keep them simple, and to focus on key concepts. However, many of the concepts that apply to directly transmitted microbial infections can also be extended to larger parasites or indirectly transmitted pathogens.

2.1 Why model infectious diseases?

It is important to state at the outset that all disease models are no more than rough representations of complex social and biological processes. Inevitably, therefore, models involve simplification, sometimes oversimplification. However there are great benefits to be derived from such a modelling approach, at both a conceptual and a practical level. Models can help us to focus on those aspects of the process of infection transmission that are in some sense fundamental, in that they help explain some of the main epidemiological features of the infection in a given population. One immediate advantage is that a single modelling framework will often apply to many different infections. For example, a model for measles will have the same structure as a model for other viral infections of childhood such as mumps and rubella, and indeed for bacterial infections such as pertussis. The insights provided by models can also have direct practical spin-offs in suggesting interventions and helping to quantify their likely impact.

The modelling approach to investigating infectious diseases can be traced back to Daniel Bernoulli, who in the 1760s became involved in an acrimonious controversy about the merits of smallpox inoculation with Jean-le-Rond D'Alembert who questioned its benefits. Bernoulli developed a model, which he applied to available data to demonstrate that inoculation resulted in reduced smallpox mortality. The basic ideas behind Bernoulli's model are much the same as those used in today's so-called **compartmental models**, which you have already met in Book 5, Chapter 3.

2.2 Compartmental models

A typical human population (say, of the UK) comprises a large number of different individuals, each of whom have their distinctive characteristics. The first stage in the modelling process is to reduce this diversity to a few key attributes deemed to be of particular relevance to the infection process. For example, for most common infections of childhood it makes sense to divide the population at any time into those that are susceptible to the infection, those that are infected, and those who have recovered from the infection and are immune.

For ease of presentation, we shall follow standard conventions and label the three compartments S (for Susceptible), I (Infected, i.e. with active infection) and R (Recovered, and hence immune to further infection). Accordingly, this model is called the **SIR model**. The letters also stand for the numbers of individuals in each compartment. To indicate that the numbers might vary over time, represented by the letter t, we write them as $S(t)$ (which, should you wish to read it out loud, is pronounced 'ess of tee'), $I(t)$ and $R(t)$.

Let N denote the total size of the population, which we shall assume is constant, so that the number of births offsets the number of deaths, and the infection has negligible associated mortality. Then:

$$N = S(t) + I(t) + R(t)$$

Note that it is assumed here that, at any point in time, every individual in the population is either susceptible (S), infected (I) or recovered (R).

◯ Which of the three compartments are children born into? Which compartment are most elderly people likely to be in?

⬤ In this model, children are born into the susceptible compartment S. Most elderly people are likely to have experienced infection at some point in the past, and hence will be in the recovered (and immune) compartment R.

As implied by the use of the time variable t, the SIR model is dynamic in that, in general, the numbers in each compartment may fluctuate over time, even though the total population size remains constant. The importance of this dynamic aspect for measles is shown in Figure 2.1. The data reveal large fluctuations in the numbers of reports of measles cases over time, prior to the introduction of measles vaccination in 1968. These recurrent epidemics are typical of many endemic infections with short infectious periods. As you will see in Chapter 5, the epidemic waves can be explained by variations in the numbers of susceptibles, $S(t)$, over time.

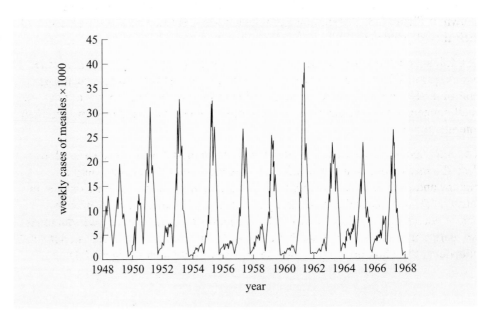

FIGURE 2.1

Weekly case notifications of measles in England and Wales for the period 1948 to 1968, prior to the introduction of measles vaccination.

◯ The measles rash typically appears about 10–14 days after infection, but only a proportion of measles infections are reported. Deduce what a graph of $I(t)$ against time, t, might look like. Can you guess what a graph of $S(t)$ against t should look like?

⬤ The clinical signs of measles appear soon (on the scale of the graph) after infection, so $I(t)$ will mirror the fluctuations in notified cases, and look like a sequence of sharp spikes. During an epidemic, the number of susceptibles $S(t)$ will fall rapidly. Once the epidemic is over, the numbers of susceptibles will gradually build up again as they are replenished by births. Thus $S(t)$ might be expected to have a saw-tooth profile, with gradual build-ups followed by sudden drops corresponding to epidemics, as shown in Figure 2.2.

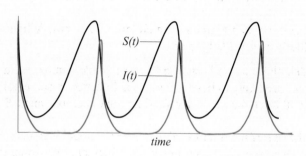

FIGURE 2.2
Idealised diagram of numbers infected, $I(t)$, and numbers susceptible, $S(t)$, for measles in the UK prior to the introduction of mass vaccination.

The SIR model is dynamic in a second sense (that is, other than in the sense that $S(t)$, $I(t)$ and $R(t)$ vary over time): individuals are born susceptible, then might acquire infection, from which they then recover. Thus each individual typically progresses over time from susceptible, to infected, to recovered. This individual dynamic aspect is often represented by means of a flow diagram in which boxes represent the susceptible, infected and recovered compartments, and arrows between them represent the transitions between the different compartments, as shown in Figure 2.3. For simplicity, the boxes are identified as S, I and R, shorn of their time dependence.

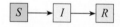

FIGURE 2.3
Flow diagram for the SIR model.

In a full specification of the model, it is also necessary to specify *transition rates*, which quantify how many individuals are transferred between compartments per unit time. These transition rates are described in subsequent sections. For now we shall concentrate on the structure of the model, namely the compartments and their interrelationships.

The SIR model is a very useful and versatile basic model, which can be used to describe many infections that confer long-lasting immunity, such as measles, mumps and rubella. It can of course be elaborated in many ways. For example, in many infections, individuals go through a *latent period* after they are infected, before becoming infectious. This can be accommodated by including an additional compartment E denoting the number *exposed* to infection and infected but not yet infectious; the I box now represents the infectious individuals (Figure 2.4).

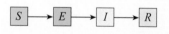

FIGURE 2.4
Flow diagram for the SEIR model.

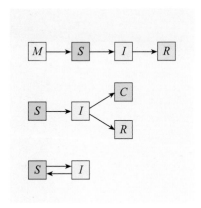

FIGURE 2.5

Flow diagrams for three compartmental models:
(a) SIR model with maternally protected class M;
(b) SIR model with carrier state C;
(c) SIS model.

○ Develop compartmental models with the following features, and draw their flow diagrams. (a) For many infections, such as measles, babies are not born susceptible but with maternal antibodies which protect them for a few months after birth. Introduce a new compartment M to represent babies with maternally-derived immunity. (b) For diseases such as hepatitis B, acute infection can lead either to recovery or to a life-long carrier state. Introduce a new carrier compartment C distinct from the recovered class. (c) Some infections, for example those responsible for the common cold, do not confer any long-lasting immunity. Such infections do not possess a recovered state R; infectious individuals become susceptible again after infection.

● Suitable flow diagrams are shown in Figure 2.5. For (c), the model is often referred to as SIS, for Susceptible-Infected-Susceptible.

2.3 Transmission risks and rates

The key feature of infectious diseases, which sets them apart from other diseases, is that they can be acquired by contact with infectious agents. As previously, we restrict attention to infectious agents directly transmitted between humans, i.e. by direct person-to-person contact.

Transmission of infection requires three conditions: presence of an infectious individual, presence of a susceptible individual, and effective contact between them. An **effective contact** is defined as contact between two individuals A and B such that, if A is infectious and B susceptible, then A infects B. What constitutes an effective contact depends on the infectious agent and its route of transmission. Some of the most important **routes of transmission** (see also Book 2 and Book 5) for directly transmitted infectious agents include:

respiratory: this is the typical mode of transmission of many infectious agents such as those causing measles, mumps, rubella, whooping cough, influenza, tuberculosis, all of which can be transmitted by airborne droplets.

faecal-oral: this is the typical transmission mode for the infectious agents of polio, hepatitis A, rotavirus, cholera, for example, either by direct contact or through contaminated foodstuffs or water.

sexual: the typical mode of transmission of the infectious agents of AIDS, syphilis, gonorrhoea, hepatitis B.

vertical: from mother to child, often *in utero*, as may occur with HIV and hepatitis B viruses.

Many infections are transmitted by more than one route: for example close physical contact plays a role in passing on the measles virus as well as transmission by airborne droplets; polio viruses can be transmitted by the respiratory route as well as by the faecal-oral route; hepatitis B virus can be transmitted by injecting drug use as well as by sexual contact. Other modes of transmission include **iatrogenic** transmission, that is, transmission caused by medical procedures, such as injection or transplantation of infected material. An example of the latter is transmission of Creutzfeldt Jakob Disease through injection of contaminated growth hormone or corneal transplants. See also Book 1, Chapter 4, on hospital-acquired infections.

The route of transmission is important from an epidemiological standpoint, because contact patterns in a given population typically depend on socio-economic, cultural and other features of the population, which may vary between different populations, and between different social groups within populations. For example, overcrowded housing and large family sizes may result in increased contact rates for many infections, such as tuberculosis. Low personal and food hygiene due to lack of availability of clean running water may result in increased polio transmission. Differences in incidence of disease between different social groups can illuminate causes and suggest interventions, as for example with human papilloma virus and cervical cancer (Box 2.1).

Box 2.1 Human papillomavirus (HPV) infection and cervical cancer

A century ago, epidemiologists noted that cervical cancer was common in female sex workers but very rare in nuns – except for nuns who had been sexually active before entering the convent. They also observed high risks of cervical cancer in women married to men whose first wives had died of cervical cancer. From this epidemiological evidence, it could be deduced that cervical cancer was caused by a sexually-transmitted infectious agent. In the 1970s, this agent was identified as human papillomavirus (HPV), already known to cause cutaneous and genital warts. It has since been demonstrated that HPV is implicated in over 90% of cervical cancers. (See also Book 2.)

Despite advances in methods for detecting and treating cervical cancer, this disease remains a leading cause of cancer death. In the United States in 1997, for example, 14 500 cases of invasive cervical cancer were diagnosed, and nearly 5000 women died. Developing a safe and effective vaccine against HPV could thus have an enormous public health impact.

Patterns over time can also reflect shifts in contact patterns. One example is chickenpox in the UK (Figure 2.6), a viral infection caused by the varicella zoster virus.

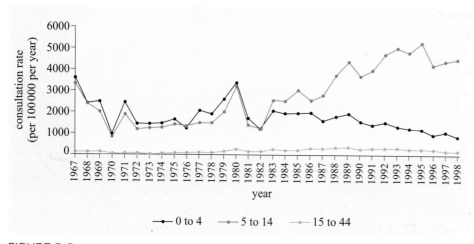

FIGURE 2.6 Annual chickenpox consultation rate by age group and year, England and Wales 1967–98.

○ Compare the rates shown in Figure 2.6 for 0–4 and 5–14 year-olds. What do you observe? Varicella zoster is transmitted by close personal contact and airborne droplets. What explanation(s) for the pattern of the data might this suggest?

◑ The consultation rates follow broadly similar patterns in the two age groups up to the early 1980s, from which point they diverge, the consultation rates in 0–4 year-olds increasing markedly thereafter. The divergent trends suggest that contact rates with 0–4 year-olds may have increased since the 1980s. This has been attributed to the increase in the proportion of children attending pre-school in the UK over this period, resulting in increased contact rates within the 0–4 year age group.

The factors influencing the effective contact rates can themselves be explored. Suppose that the effective contact rate for a given infection in a given population is denoted by the Greek letter β (beta, pronounced 'bee-tah'), measured in contacts per unit time. This may be expressed as the total contact rate, γ (gamma), multiplied by the risk of infection from contact with an infective, p. The quantity p is also called the *transmission risk*. Thus:

$$\beta = \gamma \times p$$

The contact rate, γ, will generally be greater than the effective contact rate, β, since not all contacts between an infective and a susceptible individual result in transmission of infection. The point of introducing this further complication is to formalise the fact that the effective contact rate depends not just on the social contact patterns, represented by γ, but also on the specific contexts in which contacts occur and the biology of the infective organism, both of which influence the transmission risk, p. For example, it is known that presence of a concurrent sexually transmitted infection can substantially increase the per-contact infection risk of HIV (and hence the value of p). Hence one way to reduce HIV transmission is to treat other sexually transmitted diseases, and thus reduce the value of p.

Measuring contact rates accurately is extremely difficult in general, whatever the route of transmission, not least because contact rates typically vary between individuals and groups, and can seldom be documented accurately. For sexually transmitted infections, large scale population surveys of sexual behaviour have been conducted to estimate the contact rate, γ (see Box 1.1 above).

○ Researchers have attempted to measure the contact rate γ relevant to infections transmitted by airborne droplets, like measles and whooping cough, by using conversations in lieu of contacts. Is this approach likely to work?

◑ The problem is that other relevant contacts, such as those made with fellow passengers on a bus, colleagues at work or fellow cinema-goers, will not be documented. A 'relevant contact' here could simply involve breathing in infected droplets from a person sneezing (Figure 2.7). Nevertheless, the method might perhaps provide information on the relative sizes of the contact rates in different age groups.

Ethical considerations generally preclude direct experimentation to establish per-contact infection risks, since they would require individuals to be knowingly exposed to infectious agents. However there are some notable exceptions, such as

FIGURE 2.7
Droplet dispersal following a violent sneeze.

the experiments conducted by the Common Cold Unit in the UK (see Box 2.2). Transmission risk, p, can nevertheless be estimated in certain circumstances when exposures to infection are documented, as with needlestick injuries (puncturing the skin with the needle of a syringe) among health workers involving contaminated blood products.

Box 2.2   The Common Cold Unit

Common colds account for over a third of all acute respiratory infections in humans, and carry substantial economic costs from days off work. Rhinoviruses are responsible for about 30% of common colds, and coronaviruses for 10%. Many other infectious agents cause symptoms indistinguishable from those caused by rhinoviruses and coronaviruses.

In 1946, the Medical Research Council in the UK set up the Common Cold Unit on Salisbury Plain to undertake laboratory and epidemiological research. Volunteers were recruited to take part in experiments on the transmission and treatment of the common cold. In 1965, human coronaviruses were first isolated from volunteers at the Unit.

Advertisements for volunteers were placed in newspapers and magazines. They were paid a small amount, and a stay at the Unit was presented as an unusual holiday opportunity. Volunteers usually stayed for ten days, and were housed in twos and threes, but were strictly isolated from others during their stay.

The last batch of volunteers left the Common Cold Unit in 1989, ending a unique chapter in the study of infectious diseases. Unfortunately, a cure for the common cold remains elusive.

One of the few opportunities for a more direct assessment of transmission risks is provided by *contact studies*, sometimes carried out in the context of an outbreak. The first case (the primary case) within a defined group such as a family unit is identified. Cases infected by the primary case (these are called secondary cases) are documented. If the number of susceptibles within the group is denoted n, and the number of secondary cases is x, then an estimate of the transmission risk in conditions of close contact is represented by $p = x/n$, sometimes called the *secondary attack rate* (it is really a risk, not a rate, but the term is commonly used nonetheless). Note that, even if the whole group were susceptible, x is generally less than the reproduction number R_0. This is because R_0 includes *all* secondary cases, not just those occurring within the group surveyed. For example, secondary attack rates might be calculated within families, and thus ignore any secondary cases outside the family group.

Usually, data are aggregated over several groups. For example, suppose that in a measles outbreak, primary cases are identified in five families with, respectively 3, 1, 1, 2, 2 children who have not had measles, and that the numbers of secondary cases within these five families are, respectively, 2, 0, 1, 1, 0. The total number of susceptible children exposed is $3 + 1 + 1 + 2 + 2 = 9$, and the total number of secondary cases is $2 + 0 + 1 + 1 + 0 = 4$. Hence the secondary attack rate is

$$p = \frac{4}{9} \approx 0.44$$

There are inevitably many complications with such calculations. For example, determining who is susceptible often relies on tenuous evidence; distinguishing secondary cases (that is, those directly infected by the primary case) from subsequent cases (for example tertiary cases, namely those infected by the secondaries) can be difficult, and it has to be assumed that infections from outside the group can be ignored. Nevertheless, family contact studies can be used for comparing transmission risks of different infectious agents. They are also used to compare secondary attack rates in vaccinated and unvaccinated family members, and hence in assessing the efficacy of vaccines in reducing transmission risks.

Table 2.1 Numbers of children exposed to a primary case of whooping cough and numbers of secondary cases of whooping cough, by diphtheria-tetanus-pertussis (DTP) vaccination status.

	Secondary cases	Exposed children
DTP-vaccinated	452	1937
DTP-unvaccinated	1528	2479

○ The data in Table 2.1 are from a study of whooping cough vaccine efficacy in conditions of household exposure. Calculate the secondary attack rates in the DTP vaccinated group (p_v), and in the DTP-unvaccinated group (p_u), assuming that all exposed children were susceptible. Compare the rates in the two groups. What do you conclude about the effect of vaccination?

● The secondary attack rate in the DTP-vaccinated group is $p_v = 452 / 1937 \approx 0.233$. In the DTP-unvaccinated group it is $p_u = 1528 / 2479 \approx 0.616$. This is much higher than in the vaccinated group: vaccination appears to confer protection against whooping cough in conditions of household exposure.

2.4 Homogeneous mixing

For much of the remainder of Book 6, we will make the simplifying assumption that contacts occur *at random* in the population. This is known as **homogeneous mixing**. The homogeneous mixing assumption is usually an oversimplification: in reality, contact rates typically vary with age, social status, location, gender and so on. However, assuming homogeneous mixing greatly simplifies technical details, thus bringing out the relationships between the various epidemiological parameters. Furthermore, all the main concepts illustrated in the simplified setting of homogeneous mixing also apply in the more general, and realistic, case of **heterogeneous mixing**. In Section 4.4 we will briefly discuss the implications of relaxing this and other simplifying assumptions.

Under the homogeneous mixing assumption we can derive a simple relationship between the effective contact rate β and the basic reproduction number, R_0, which was introduced in Chapter 1. Recall that R_0 is the average number of secondary infections resulting from contact with a single typical infective introduced in a totally susceptible population. Assuming homogeneous mixing means that we need not worry about how to define what constitutes a 'typical' infective: all infectives are equivalent from the point of view of transmission.

Suppose that effective contacts occur randomly at a rate β in this population, and that the average duration of the infectious period is D. Then the total number of effective contacts made by one infectious individual is $\beta \times D$. But if the entire population is susceptible, then each one of these effective contacts results in an infection (by definition of what an effective contact is). Hence the number of secondary infections is also equal to $\beta \times D$, and hence we obtain the relationship:

$$R_0 = \beta \times D$$

This gives a flavour of the relationships between parameters that will be derived in subsequent sections.

2.5 The force of infection

As indicated in the previous section, transmission rates, though fundamental to our understanding of infectious diseases, are difficult to estimate. The difficulty is due to the fact that it is not usually possible to document all contacts. For some relatively uncommon yet serious infectious diseases, such as tuberculosis and AIDS in developed countries, much effort is devoted to *contact tracing,* namely identifying contacts of cases in order to control the spread of infection. For most infections, however, such an exercise is impractical.

It is considerably easier, however, to calculate *incidence rates* of infections, that is, the rates at which individuals become infected. For example, if in a given city of, say, 100 000 inhabitants, 800 cases of measles are observed over a six-month period (i.e. 0.5 year), then an estimate of the (annual) incidence rate of measles is simply

$$\text{incidence rate} = \frac{800}{100\,000 \times 0.5} = 0.016 \text{ per year}$$

Clearly, as discussed in Section 1.3, there are all kinds of practical difficulties with such calculations, since not all cases are reported, and not all infections produce clinical symptoms. Since clinical disease is usually the trigger for a case to consult a doctor, subclinical or mild cases will not be included in official statistics.

☐ Suppose that 50% of infections with *Bordetella pertussis* produce typical symptoms, and that on average general practitioners notify only 25% of the typical whooping cough cases they see. Calculate the proportion of infections that are notified as whooping cough cases. What other major source of inaccuracy might affect notification data, and how will it affect the incidence rate?

⬤ The proportion of infections included in the whooping cough notifications is $0.5 \times 0.25 = 0.125$, or 12.5%. Another source of inaccuracy in notification data stems from the fact that diagnoses are often based on clinical criteria, which may be non-specific. For example, other infectious agents may produce similar clinical symptoms to *Bordetella pertussis*. Non-specificity of clinical diagnoses will tend to *exaggerate* incidence.

However, a more fundamental shortcoming of incidence rates is that they do not reflect *transmission* rates; this is because they take no account of *susceptibility.* Consider for instance the following example: a family includes five people, two adults and three children aged 6 months, 2 years and 5 years. None of the family is vaccinated against measles. The 5-year-old develops measles. The other four members of the family can be assumed to be equally exposed to the measles virus in the home, from contacts with the infectious 5-year-old. However, secondary cases can occur only among susceptibles. The two adults are likely already to have had measles, and hence to be immune: if so, they are not susceptible. The two children, on the other hand, are quite likely not to have had measles, and hence will be susceptible. Thus if infection spreads in the family, the children are more likely than the adults to become infected, even though the contact rates are the same for all members of the family.

○ Table 2.2 and Figure 2.8 show the age distribution of notified measles cases in England and Wales for a period prior to the introduction of measles vaccination in 1968. In what age groups is the annual incidence of measles highest? What else might you wish to know in order to compare transmission rates in different age groups?

● Note that the histogram in Figure 2.8 has varying bar widths in order to allow for the different age group widths. The incidence increases with age to a peak in 4 year-olds, then declines. It is important to remember that these data are based on *notifications*, and that completeness of notifications might vary with age. However, it is perhaps unlikely that it would vary quite enough to explain the big differences in incidence shown in Figure 2.8. Nevertheless, we cannot immediately conclude that the transmission rate is higher among 5–9 year-olds than among 10–14 year-olds, say, since many more 10–14 year-olds than 5–9 year-olds are likely to be immune.

Table 2.2
Measles notifications by age, England and Wales 1956–1965.

Age group (years)	Notifications
0	221 267
1	424 616
2	544 251
3	580 855
4	595 364
5–9	1 868 340
10–14	109 937
15–24	26 790
25+	15 855
All	4 387 275

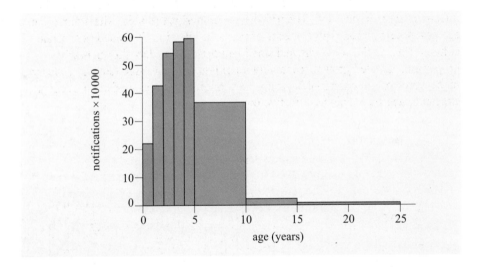

FIGURE 2.8 Histogram of measles notifications in individuals aged < 25 years, England and Wales 1956–1965.

Some elaboration of the notion of incidence rate is required to take account of susceptibility, and so allow comparisons to be made between different subgroups of the population, and in particular between different age groups.

The concept we need is the **force of infection**. The force of infection is the rate at which *susceptible* individuals become infected, and will be denoted by λ (lambda). It can be calculated in much the same way as an incidence rate, except that the denominator population used in the calculation includes only susceptible individuals: immunes are excluded from the denominator.

○ Cytomegalovirus (CMV) infection in pregnancy can cause hearing loss, visual impairment, and neurological problems in the child. These problems appear to occur primarily in the babies of women not previously infected. Data from the USA suggest that about 70% of women of childbearing age have been infected. It is estimated that about 2% of pregnant women first become infected with CMV during pregnancy. Calculate the annual incidence rate and the annual force of CMV infection in pregnant women in the USA.

● Since pregnancy lasts 9/12 = 0.75 year, and 2% = 2/100, the incidence rate is

$$\frac{2}{100 \times 0.75} \approx 0.027 \text{ per year}$$

Out of 100 pregnant women, about 30 have not had a prior CMV infection. So the average annual force of infection, λ, is

$$\lambda = \frac{2}{30 \times 0.75} \approx 0.089$$

Unlike the incidence rate, the force of infection λ is directly proportional to the effective transmission rate β, and hence it makes sense to compare forces of infection in different subgroups of a population, in different populations and even between infections. This may be done directly using serological surveys: the higher the force of infection, the greater the rate at which susceptibles become infected, and hence the steeper the rise in the proportion of the population with specific antibodies against the infectious agent in question. The proportion seropositive (that is, with antibody) in each age group (and hence, with evidence of previous infection) is plotted as separate columns for people from large and small families. Figure 2.9a shows that the proportions infected grow more rapidly for children within large families, reflecting the higher force of infection in this group. This in turn is the result of more frequent exposure, and hence higher effective contact rates.

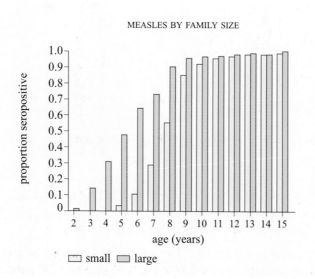

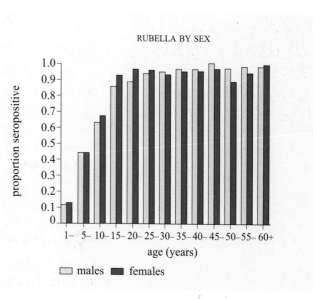

FIGURE 2.9 Serological data by age: (a) measles, by family size: USA, 1957; (b) rubella, by sex: England, 1980–84

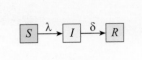

FIGURE 2.10

The SIR model with transition rates λ (the force of infection) and δ.

Caution is required in interpreting serological data in the presence of vaccination, since both natural infection and vaccination elicit an antibody response. Figure 2.9b, for example, shows the proportions with rubella antibody by age and sex in the UK in 1980–84. The small excess of seropositives in females aged 10–25 years is most probably the result of the selective rubella vaccination programme for girls which was in operation at the time.

In terms of the SIR model of Section 2.2, the force of infection is the *transition rate* at which individuals move from the susceptible compartment to the infected compartment. To fully describe the SIR model, it only remains to specify δ (the Greek symbol delta), the *transition rate* between the infected and the recovered classes. Since the infectious period is D, an individual experiences 1 recovery in D units of time. Hence the rate at which infectious individuals recover is $\delta = 1/D$. The fully specified SIR model, complete with transition rates, is shown in Figure 2.10.

Summary of Chapter 2

1   Compartmental models such as the SIR model provide a simple framework that can help focus on the key stages of infectious disease transmission.

2   For directly transmitted infections, the types of contacts that are relevant in transmission are determined by the route of transmission. Contact rates are difficult to estimate directly in most settings.

3   The force of infection is the rate at which susceptibles become infected. The force of infection is important because it can be estimated more easily than contact rates, particularly under the assumption of homogeneous mixing, which assumes that contacts occur at random within the population.

3 ENDEMIC INFECTIONS

In the last section you saw that the transmission rate β is directly related to the basic reproduction number R_0 through the relation

$$R_0 = \beta \times D$$

where D is the average duration of the infectious period. It was also pointed out that in most circumstances it is rather difficult to estimate β. In this chapter we shall consider an important setting in which it is possible to estimate R_0 directly for some endemic infections.

3.1 The endemic steady state

An infection is said to be **endemic** in a given population if the infection is maintained within that population without the need for external inputs. For example, parvovirus B19 infection is endemic in the UK, malaria is not. Each year, there are a few instances of malaria acquired in the UK, but these do not lead to sustained transmission within the UK population. In other words, malaria cannot currently become established in the UK: the value of R_0 for malaria in the UK is very much less than 1. This situation could change if, for example, climate change led to conditions in which *Anopheles* mosquitoes were to flourish.

Provided the population is sufficiently large (see Box 3.1), endemicity can be maintained by sustained person-to-person transmission, for which the necessary condition is $R_0 > 1$, or by the presence of a suitable animal reservoir.

In a large population, infections with $R_0 > 1$ become endemic and coexist in ecological balance with the host population. If the contact rates, transmission probabilities and the size of the host population remain broadly constant over a long period, then the number of infections per unit time will eventually settle down and fluctuate in regular seasonal or epidemic cycles around an average level. We shall refer to such an infection as being in an **endemic steady state**.

For example, infections such as whooping cough, measles, mumps and rubella are endemic infections that were roughly in a steady state in the UK, prior to the introduction of mass vaccination. In reality, no infection is ever exactly in a steady state since there are inevitably small fluctuations in the numbers of births and contact patterns. However the steady state concept is useful and serves to describe the long-term regularity observed in many time series of infectious diseases. Figure 3.1, for example, shows the incidence rate of chickenpox in France

FIGURE 3.1
Chickenpox incidence rate, France, 1991–2001.

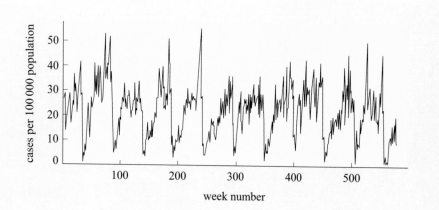

over time. The rate varies seasonally around an average that remains broadly constant: it is reasonable to conclude that varicella-zoster infection in France was in a steady state over this period.

Box 3.1   Stochastic extinction

An infection with $R_0 > 1$ can become extinct if there are insufficient numbers of susceptibles to maintain transmission. This is because the numbers of infectious individuals typically oscillate over time, giving rise to epidemic cycles (epidemic cycles are discussed in more detail in Chapter 5). During a trough, the number of infectious individuals can become zero as a result of chance fluctuations. If this happens, there are no more infectious individuals left to transmit the infection, which then dies out until new infections are imported. This is the phenomenon of *stochastic extinction*. The likelihood of stochastic extinction occurring increases as the population size gets smaller. Small, isolated island populations provide the ideal setting in which to study this phenomenon. Figure 3.2 shows the pattern of measles epidemics in Iceland prior to mass vaccination. Epidemics are set off by infected visitors to the island; between epidemics, no cases occur.

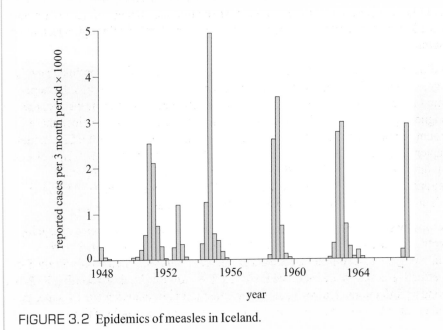

FIGURE 3.2 Epidemics of measles in Iceland.

○ Consider another example. Is HIV endemic in Europe? In Southern Africa? Is it in a steady state in either of these regions? (Think back to the HIV case study associated with Book 3.)

● HIV is endemic both in Europe and in Southern Africa: the transmission of HIV is sustained within both regions, even though the epidemiology of HIV differs. For example in Southern Africa most transmission is within the heterosexual population, whereas in Europe sustained transmission occurs mainly within male homosexual and intravenous drug-using populations. However, in neither region has HIV reached a steady state, owing partly to its long infectious period, often lasting many years.

The average steady state level reached by an infection may be interpreted in terms of average transmission rates. If an infection has reached an endemic steady state, then each infectious individual will infect, on average, exactly one other individual. Clearly the numbers actually infected depend on the epidemic cycle. But the *average* number, that is the number of secondary infections averaged over several epidemic cycles, must be equal to one.

To see why this must be so, suppose that on average, an infectious individual infects more than one other. Suppose, for definiteness, that an infectious individual infects on average two others. Then each of these infects, on average, two as well, making four; each of these infects two, making eight, and so on. The implication is that the average incidence must rise exponentially over time (see Figure 1.3). But this contradicts the fact that the incidence fluctuates around a constant average level, since the infection is endemic and in a steady state. A similar argument applies if each infectious individual infects, on average, *fewer* than one individual (so that, for instance, two infectious individuals infect, on average, only one other). In this situation, the average incidence should decline, again in contradiction with the observed steady state.

> An exponential change is one in which the value of a quantity decreases or increases by the same factor in equal intervals.

This 'average' steady state level can be quantified by the average proportion of the population that are immune. This is called the **herd immunity level** (or population immunity level). As you will see in the next section, the concept of herd immunity plays a key role in strategies to control infections, particularly through vaccination programmes.

Let S denote the average proportion of the population that are susceptible. This is roughly equal to 1 minus the proportion who are immune, i.e. 1 minus the herd immunity level. The 'roughly' in the previous sentence comes from the fact that we are ignoring those with active infection. However this is reasonable since these account for only a small proportion of the population. In terms of the SIR model of Chapter 2, the average proportion susceptible S is the average value of $S(t)$ over a long interval of time t. Now follows a little logic, from which an important relationship between R_0 and S will emerge. The argument is expressed through mathematical equations; making sense of these is discussed in Box 3.2.

In a wholly susceptible population, an infectious individual makes on average R_0 effective contacts. Now consider what happens if only a proportion S of the population are susceptible. If contacts are made at random, then a proportion S of the effective contacts are made with susceptible individuals, thus resulting in $R_0 \times S$ secondary infections. However, since the infection is in endemic steady state, this number must be equal to one. We thus have the important relationship:

$$R_0 \times S = 1$$

for an infection in endemic steady state for which contacts occur at random. The importance of this relationship may be grasped from the fact that it may also be written

$$R_0 = \frac{1}{S}$$

In other words, provided that it is possible to determine the proportion susceptible, it is also possible to calculate the basic reproduction number (provided that contacts occur at random).

Box 3.2   Making sense of mathematical equations

The first thing to do when confronted with a mathematical equation is to look at it and make sure you understand what it is saying. For example, the equation

$$R_0 \times S = 1$$

means that if you multiply the reproduction number, R_0, with the proportion susceptible, S, you *must* get 1. Here R_0 is the reproduction number of an endemic infection, so it must be greater than 1, while S is a proportion, so it must be less than 1. So, for example, if $R_0 = 3$, then $S = 1/3$. Or if $S = 0.2$, then $R_0 = 5$.

You might then ask yourself, so what? The reason this equation is important (and worth spending some time on) is that R_0 is an important quantity. However, its definition is rather theoretical (see Section 1.2), and it's far from clear how to calculate R_0 in practice. This equation ties it to S in a very direct way: if you know S, you must also know R_0 (at least for homogeneously mixing populations). And the beauty is that S is relatively *easy* to estimate.

The next equation makes this explicit:

$$R_0 = \frac{1}{S}$$

This is obtained from the previous equation by dividing both sides by S. The advantage of this second expression is that it puts the relationship in a directly useable form. Given an estimate of S, you can substitute for it in the equation and read off the value of R_0. Thus, if $S = 0.5$, $R_0 = 1/0.5 = 2$.

For example, suppose that it is found that 93% of a large, homogeneously mixing population are immune to measles. Since $S = 1 - 0.93 = 0.07$, it follows that

$$R_0 = \frac{1}{S}$$

$$= \frac{1}{0.07} \approx 14.3$$

Thus the basic reproduction number for measles in this population is about 14. This means that, if the population were wholly susceptible, then one infectious individual in this population would infect, on average, about 14 others.

☐ Suppose that 62% of a large, homogeneously mixing population are immune to hepatitis A virus infection. Calculate the basic reproduction number for hepatitis A infection in this population.

⬤ $S = 1 - 0.62 = 0.38$. Hence

$$R_0 = \frac{1}{0.38} \approx 2.6$$

Thus, if the population were wholly susceptible, then one case infected with hepatitis A virus would infect, on average, 2.6 others.

At this point, you might be wondering why bother to calculate R_0 for endemic infectious agents, since the actual population is certainly not 'completely susceptible' as required in the definition of R_0. The reason is that R_0 summarises the infectious potential of the infective agent in this population, which depends on the agent, its infectious period, and the rate at which effective contacts occur in the population. As you will learn in Chapter 4, this in turn is used to quantify the vaccination level required to eliminate infection.

☐ Consider an infection in the endemic steady state. It might appear more relevant to calculate the average number of cases directly infected by a single infectious case *in the actual population in which the infectious agent is endemic*, rather than in an abstract 'completely susceptible' equivalent population. Use the logic of this section to explain why this is not the case.

⬤ The reason is that, for an infectious agent in the endemic steady state, the average number of cases directly infected by one case must be equal to 1. This is true of all endemic infectious agents, and so this apparently more 'relevant' quantity is in fact of no use at all for contrasting different infectious agents.

3.2 The average age at infection

In the previous section, we reduced the problem of estimating R_0 to that of estimating the proportion susceptible, S, assuming homogeneous mixing. In this section we simplify the problem even further, and show how S, and hence R_0, can sometimes be calculated from an even simpler quantity, the **average age at infection**, A. The advantage of this is that the average age at infection can be calculated directly from case reports.

The average age at infection is, as its name indicates, the average age at which individuals in the population become infected. The average age at infection is an important parameter and is related to the force of infection, λ, by

$$A = \frac{1}{\lambda}$$

To understand this equation, think of A as the average time spent in the susceptible compartment. The rate at which susceptibles are infected is then $1/A$. Thus, $\lambda = 1/A$ and so $A = 1/\lambda$.

A similar argument was used at the end of Section 2.5 to obtain the transition rate δ in the SIR model.

The average age at infection provides a direct way of comparing forces of infection in different sub-populations, or between different infections in the same population. For example, if it is known that the average age at infection of measles is, say, 4 years and that of rubella is, say, 6 years, then you can infer immediately that, on average, the force of infection for measles is higher than that for rubella.

The average age at infection is also critical in the design of control strategies, as will be seen in greater detail in the next section. Thus, for a vaccination programme to be effective, it must be targeted at individuals *below* the average age at infection. For example, if the average age at infection of measles in a given population is 3 years, then relying solely on vaccination at school entry at ages 4–5 years will only have a marginal impact on measles virus transmission (though of course early vaccination followed by a booster at school entry makes sense).

◯ In a given population, the average age at infection by hepatitis A virus is 22 years. It is proposed to control hepatitis A virus by mass vaccination of teenagers. Is this likely to work?

⬤ A teenage mass vaccination programme is a reasonable contender as it would be targeted at individuals below the average age at infection. (There may of course be other problems associated with vaccinating at that age, such as how to ensure high vaccination coverage.)

Since the force of infection and the average age at infection are related to the endemic steady state, you might expect them to be related also to the herd immunity level. As indeed they are. In order to elucidate the relationship, however, it is necessary to be more specific about the age distribution in the population.

Age distributions, and mortality rates, vary greatly between countries. We will consider two contrasting hypothetical scenarios, illustrated in Figure 3.3:

Scenario 1

Everybody lives to the same age L, and then dies (in Figure 3.3, deaths occur at 75 years). Under this scenario, the age distribution is said to be rectangular: the mortality rate is zero to age L, and then everybody dies.

Scenario 2

The mortality rate is the same at each age. This gives rise to an *exponential* age distribution, with fewer older people than younger people. The average age in the population is L (in Figure 3.3, this is 75 years).

In both scenarios, L is also known as the *life expectancy* (or *expectation of life*) at birth.

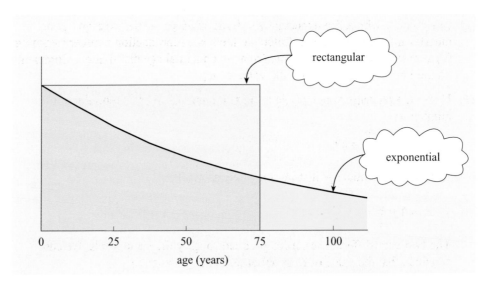

FIGURE 3.3
Rectangular and exponential age distributions with the same life expectancy $L = 75$ years.

Both scenarios are unrealistic, and in most cases the true situation will lie somewhere in between. Countries with low infant mortality, in the developed world, will lie closer to scenario 1, whereas developing countries with high infant mortality will be closer to scenario 2. The point is, however, that for childhood infections, the values of R_0 obtained under the two scenarios are quite similar. In other words, the precise details of the age distribution are not critical.

Suppose that the age distribution is rectangular, so that everybody lives to age L, the life expectancy, and dies. If the average age at infection is A, then *on average* individuals aged less than A are susceptible, and those aged greater than A are either immune or infectious, as shown in Figure 3.4. Thus the proportion of the population who are susceptible is

$$S = \frac{A}{L}$$

Thus, in such a population,

$$R_0 = \frac{1}{S}$$

$$= \frac{1}{(A/L)}$$

$$= \frac{L}{A}$$

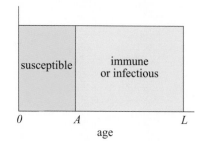

FIGURE 3.4

Relationship between S, A and L in a population with rectangular age structure.

For a population with exponential age structure, the argument is a little more complicated and will be omitted. Under the exponential age distribution assumption of scenario 2, it turns out that

$$R_0 = 1 + \frac{L}{A}$$

This differs by only 1 from the value obtained under the assumption of a rectangular age distribution. In other words, provided you know the average age at infection and the life expectancy, you can estimate the basic reproduction number, and need not worry unduly about the age distribution of the population.

☐ In a country with a life expectancy at birth of 60 years, the average age at measles infection is 3 years. Calculate the basic reproduction number assuming (a) a rectangular age distribution, (b) an exponential age distribution. Comment on the impact of mortality on the value of R_0.

⬤ Under the rectangular age distribution assumption, the basic reproduction number is:

$$R_0 = \frac{L}{A} = \frac{60}{3} = 20$$

Under the exponential age distribution assumption, it is:

$$R_0 = 1 + \frac{L}{A} = 1 + \frac{60}{3} = 21$$

The two very different scenarios produce roughly the same result. We can conclude that the value of R_0 is about 20 in this population.

3.3 Estimation from epidemiological data

From earlier sections, we know that for infections in an endemic steady state in large homogeneously mixing populations, the basic reproduction number R_0 can be estimated provided that either the average proportion susceptible, S, or the average age at infection, A, are known, along with the life expectancy L.

The life expectancy (and the age structure of the population) can often be obtained from published data for the population, or estimated from separate surveys. The proportion susceptible S and the average age at infection A, however, must be estimated from epidemiological data. This can be done using data from a serological survey.

3.3.1 Estimation from serological survey data

The method is best illustrated using a practical example. Table 3.1 shows data from a serological survey of hepatitis A virus infection in Bulgaria. As in many surveys, only a small proportion of the whole population is surveyed. Provided that the sample is representative, however, we can draw inferences about the population as a whole from this sample.

Table 3.1 Numbers tested and positive for hepatitis A antibodies, Bulgaria.

Age group (years)	Tested	Positive
1–10	135	46
11–20	160	66
21–30	133	97
31–40	116	94
41–50	101	96
51–60	101	96
61–70	61	59

Hepatitis A virus is transmitted by the faecal-oral route, through direct contact or ingestion of contaminated food. The data are aggregated in seven 10-year age groups, and Table 3.1 gives the numbers tested in each age group, and the numbers positive, that is, with IgG antibodies to hepatitis A virus. For hepatitis A virus, a positive test result indicates immunity. Thus the proportions positive in each age group estimate the proportion immune.

For some infections, such as influenza, the presence of antibodies may not indicate immunity.

In order to estimate S, the overall proportion of the population that are susceptible to hepatitis A virus infection, the first step is to calculate the proportion susceptible within each age group. To do this, first calculate the proportion who are immune. For example, the proportion of 1–10-year-olds who are immune is

$$\frac{46}{135} \approx 0.341$$

It then follows that the proportion of susceptibles in the 1–10 age group is

$$1 - 0.341 \approx 0.659$$

Table 3.2 shows the proportions immune and susceptible within each 10-year age group in this survey.

Table 3.2 Proportions immune and susceptible to hepatitis A virus by age, Bulgaria.

Age group (years)	Proportion immune	Proportion susceptible
1–10	0.341	0.659
11–20	0.413	0.587
21–30	0.729	0.271
31–40	0.810	0.190
41–50	0.950	0.050
51–60	0.950	0.050
61–70	0.967	0.033

Note that we are missing the data for infants; we shall assume that all infants are protected by maternal antibodies and hence the proportion susceptible among them is zero. This assumption makes the calculations easier but is probably incorrect; however it has little bearing on the final result since infants only account for a small proportion of the population.

☐ Check that you can derive the values in Table 3.2 from those in Table 3.1. What do you notice about the age trend in the proportion immune? How might you explain this? What assumption have you made?

⬤ The proportion immune increases with age. The reason for this is that older people have had more time to become infected than younger people. Note that this interpretation relies rather heavily on the assumption that hepatitis A virus infection is in endemic steady state in Bulgaria. An alternative explanation is that the force of hepatitis A infection has declined over time, and that the high proportions immune at older ages reflect past exposures to hepatitis at a time of high incidence.

Table 3.2 gives the proportions susceptible within each age band. In order to obtain S, the overall proportion of the population susceptible, we need to calculate a *weighted average* of these age-specific proportions, with weights proportional to the size of each age group within the population. This is needed because surveys are not random samples of the population: we cannot be sure that the proportion tested in each age group reflects the proportion of the population in that age group. If you do this, you can calculate that the proportion susceptible in this population is 0.259. (See Box 3.3 for details of the calculation).

Given an estimate of the proportion susceptible, S, you can now calculate the basic reproduction number for hepatitis A virus infection in this population.

☐ Calculate the value of R_0 for hepatitis A in Bulgaria. What assumptions have you made?

⬤ $R_0 = \dfrac{1}{S} = \dfrac{1}{0.259} \approx 3.9$

Thus, if the population were totally susceptible, one infectious case would infect, on average, about 4 others. The main assumptions behind this calculation is that the population mixes homogeneously, and that the infection is in a steady state.

Box 3.3
optional

Calculation of the proportion susceptible, S

We shall assume that the age distribution is broadly rectangular with life expectancy 71 years, and that population size is constant. With these assumptions the proportion of the population in each 10-year age band is $10/71$; the proportion of infants is $1/71$. Thus the proportion susceptible is

$$S = 0 \times \frac{1}{71} + 0.659 \times \frac{10}{71} + 0.587 \times \frac{10}{71} + \dots + 0.033 \times \frac{10}{71}$$

$$= (0.659 + 0.587 + 0.271 + 0.190 + 0.050 + 0.050 + 0.033) \times \frac{10}{71}$$

$$\approx 0.259$$

3.3.2 Estimation from case reports

The average age at infection, A, and hence R_0, can in some cases also be estimated from case reports, provided that the proportion of cases that are reported does not vary with age (so that, for example, a case in an adult is as likely to get reported as a case in a child). This is a reasonable assumption for measles, but not for infections for which the proportion of infections that produce symptoms (and hence are likely to be reported) varies with age. For example, infection by hepatitis A virus is much more likely to be symptomatic (and hence reported) in adults than in children.

Table 3.3 shows the total numbers of notifications of measles, by broad age group, in England and Wales between 1956 and 1965, that is, prior to the introduction of vaccination (you already met these data in Table 2.2).

Provided that the proportion of measles infections that are notified does not vary with age, then the proportions of notifications in each age group represent the probability of acquiring infection within that age group. For example, the proportion of all the infections that occurred within the 5–9 year age group is

$$\frac{1868340}{4387275} \approx 0.426$$

or about 42.6%. These infections occurred on average at 7.5 years of age, the midpoint of the 5–9 year age group.

Table 3.4 shows the distribution of age at infection, together with the age group midpoints. The midpoint of the 25+ age group is calculated assuming that everybody lives to age 75 and then dies.

○ What is the peak age at measles infection? (*Hint:* You need to take account of the age group width.)

● Although about 42.6% infections (rounded from 0.4259 in Table 3.4) occur in the 4–9 year age group, this spans 5 years so the average proportion per year is 8.52%, though it is probably higher at age 5 than at age 9 (since fewer children are immune at age 5 than at age 9). So the peak age at infection is probably 4 or 5 years.

Table 3.3 Measles notifications by age, England and Wales, 1956–1965.

Age group (years)	Notifications
0	221 267
1	424 616
2	544 251
3	580 855
4	595 364
5–9	1 868 340
10–14	109 937
15–24	26 790
25+	15 855
All	4 387 275

Table 3.4 Distribution of the age at measles infection.

Age group	Midpoint(years)	Proportion of infections
0	0.5	0.0504
1	1.5	0.0968
2	2.5	0.1241
3	3.5	0.1324
4	4.5	0.1357
5–9	7.5	0.4259
10–14	12.5	0.0251
15–24	20.0	0.0061
25+	50.0	0.0036

The average age at infection, A, is then calculated as the weighted average of the midpoints, the weights being the proportions of infections occurring in each age group. For these data, the average age at infection is 5.4 years. The details of the calculation are shown in Box 3.4.

◯ Calculate the value of R_0 in this population using a rectangular age distribution with $L = 75$ years. What assumptions have you made?

● $$R_0 = \frac{L}{A} = \frac{75}{5.4} \approx 13.9$$

So, if the population were entirely susceptible, a single measles case would infect, on average, about 14 others. This calculation assumes homogeneous mixing, and that the infection is in an endemic steady state.

<table>
<tr><td>Box 3.4
optional</td><td>Calculation of the average age at infection</td></tr>
</table>

The calculation is based on three assumptions: (a) in this population, everyone will eventually get infected with measles; (b) the age distribution in this population is rectangular, everyone dying at age 75 years; and (c) the proportion of cases of measles reported does not vary with age. Of these three assumptions, (c) is the most important. With these assumptions,

$$A = 0.5 \times 0.0504 + 1.5 \times 0.0968 + 2.5 \times 0.1241 + 3.5 \times 0.1324 + 4.5 \times 0.1357$$
$$+ 7.5 \times 0.4259 + 12.5 \times 0.0251 + 20 \times 0.0061 + 50 \times 0.0036$$
$$\approx 5.4 \text{ years}$$

Summary of Chapter 3

1   An infection is in endemic steady state when it is established in a population and undergoes regular fluctuations around a constant long-term average. In such a population, the proportion of the population that are immune is called the herd immunity level. For homogeneously mixing populations, the basic reproduction number can be estimated directly from the herd immunity level.

2   The basic reproduction number can also be estimated from the average age at infection in the population.

3   Serological survey data and case reports can be used to estimate the herd immunity level and the average age at infection, and hence the basic reproduction number of an infection.

4 VACCINATION

In Book 7, Chapter 3, you will learn about the preparation of vaccines and their biological effects on the body. Here, the focus is on modelling the effects of vaccination on infection rates in populations.

The first aim of a vaccination programme is to protect *individuals* directly from infection or disease. This direct effect of vaccination can be quantified by means of the **vaccine efficacy, VE**, which is the relative reduction in the risk of infection in vaccinees, p_v, compared to the risk in unvaccinated persons, p_u

$$VE = \frac{p_u - p_v}{p_u} \times 100$$

The *VE* is often quoted as a percentage (hence the × 100 multiplier). A vaccine with 100% efficacy reduces the risk of infection to zero in vaccinees. A vaccine with 0% efficacy has no effect.

☐ In Chapter 2 you calculated the secondary attack rates of whooping cough in vaccinated and unvaccinated household members (see Table 2.1). The secondary attack rate in the vaccinated group was $p_v = 452/1937 = 0.233$. In the unvaccinated group it was $p_u = 1528/2479 = 0.616$. Use the equation above to calculate the efficacy of this vaccine.

● The efficacy is

$$VE = \frac{0.616 - 0.233}{0.616} \times 100 \approx 62.2\%$$

Thus, vaccination reduces the risk of whooping cough by about 62% in vaccinees compared to unvaccinated people in conditions of household exposure to *Bordetella pertussis*.

However, individual protection is just one aspect of the impact of vaccination. In this chapter we shall consider the population effects of vaccination, in particular the impact of the vaccination programme on the herd immunity level.

The main purpose of this chapter is to demonstrate that an infection can be *eliminated* by vaccination, even if a proportion of the population remains unvaccinated. The key idea of this chapter is that of herd immunity. This term conveys the notion that the presence of immune individuals in sufficient numbers can reduce the incidence of infection in the remaining susceptibles. You have already met the herd immunity level in a population. As it turns out, if the proportion of immunes exceeds the herd immunity level then the infection can no longer persist in the population. Thus, if this threshold can be exceeded by vaccination, the infection will be eliminated.

The precise meaning of *elimination* in this context will be discussed in Section 4.3.

4.1 Herd immunity and the critical immunisation threshold

Recall that the basic reproduction number of an infection, R_0, is the average number of secondary infections generated by a single infective in a totally susceptible population. As you saw in Section 3.1, if an infection for which $R_0 > 1$ in a homogeneously mixing population has reached an endemic steady state, then the average proportion susceptible S is such that

$$R_0 \times S = 1$$

In this steady state, the average proportion susceptible is thus

$$S = \frac{1}{R_0}$$

The herd immunity level is $1 - S$ (see Section 3.1) and hence equals

$$1 - S = 1 - \frac{1}{R_0}$$

The herd immunity level describes the level of immunity of the population *before* mass vaccination is introduced. Consider now what happens if a mass vaccination programme is implemented in this population. Assume for simplicity that vaccination occurs close to birth and that some proportion q of the population are immunised. If this proportion is *less* than the pre-existing herd immunity level, the dynamics of the infection are perturbed but readjust eventually and settle down again (some of the implications of this are considered in the next section). However if the proportion of the population immunised through vaccination is *greater* than the pre-existing herd immunity level, then there are too few susceptibles left for transmission to be sustained. If there is no immigration of infected cases, then the infection eventually disappears.

Thus, the herd immunity level

$$1 - \frac{1}{R_0}$$

is a *threshold*: increasing the immunity level in the population beyond this threshold will lead to elimination of the infection. Box 4.1 contains a demonstration of this fact. (You can skip this box if you do not find mathematical arguments illuminating!)

The herd immunity threshold is also called the **critical immunisation threshold**, q_c (pronounced 'queue-see'):

$$q_c = 1 - \frac{1}{R_0}$$

This is the *minimum* proportion of the population that must be immunised at birth (or close to birth) for the infection to be eliminated.

Box 4.1 optional The critical immunisation threshold

Suppose that a proportion q of a completely susceptible, homogeneously mixing population is immunised at birth, and suppose that a single infectious individual is introduced into this partially immunised population. Then this individual infects on average

$$R = R_0 \times (1 - q)$$

other individuals. This is because, of the R_0 effective contacts this individual makes, only a proportion $1 - q$ are with susceptibles. The infection can only spread and become established if this number is greater than 1, that is, if

$$R_0 \times (1 - q) > 1$$

Dividing both sides by R_0 gives

$$1 - q > \frac{1}{R_0}$$

Now add q to both sides:

$$1 > \frac{1}{R_0} + q$$

Finally, subtract $1/R_0$ from both sides:

$$1 - \frac{1}{R_0} > q$$

The expression on the left is the herd immunity threshold. We started off by assuming that the infection can establish itself in a population in which a proportion q are vaccinated. We have showed that, in this case, q must be less than the herd immunity threshold. The argument can be reversed: if q is greater than this threshold, that is

$$q > 1 - \frac{1}{R_0}$$

then the same argument in reverse leads to

$$R_0 \times (1 - q) < 1$$

Thus each infectious individual infects less than one other so the infection must eventually die out.

For example, suppose that in a homogeneously mixing population, the value of R_0 for measles is 20. Then the critical immunisation threshold is

$$q_c = 1 - \frac{1}{R_0} = 1 - \frac{1}{20} = 0.95$$

Thus 95% of the population must be immunised at birth in order to eliminate the infection.

☐ Calculate the critical immunisation threshold for mumps in a homogeneously mixing population, if R_0 for mumps is 12. If the efficacy of the vaccine is 90%, can the infection be eliminated using a single-dose vaccination schedule?

$$1 - \frac{1}{R_0} = 1 - \frac{1}{12} = 0.917$$

So 91.7% of the population must be immunised. However, if the vaccine is 90% effective, then even if 100% of the population are vaccinated, only 90% will be immunised (that is, protected against infection). Hence a single-dose programme cannot eliminate infection. (In Book 7, you will learn about improving the impact of the vaccination programme by repeating the immunisation at intervals.)

It should of course be noted that all these calculations rely on population averages, and assumptions such as homogeneous mixing, and so do not reflect the heterogeneity of many real populations (see Section 4.4). Nevertheless, the critical immunisation threshold provides a useful target for a mass vaccination programme. Table 4.1 is based on Table 1.1, and shows some typical values of R_0 and q_c for a range of vaccine-preventable infections.

Table 4.1 Typical values of R_0 and q_c for selected infections.

Infectious Disease	R_0	q_c (%)
measles	10–20	90–95
whooping cough	10–20	90–95
chickenpox	5–10	80–90
mumps	5–10	80–90
rubella	4–7	75–85
diphtheria	4–7	75–85
polio	4–7	75–85
smallpox	3–5	65–80

4.2 The effects of mass vaccination programmes

Mass vaccination is a large-scale intervention which disturbs the ecological balance of the infection in its host population (and, as you saw in the previous section, can drive the infection to extinction, as it did for smallpox virus). The ultimate goal of some vaccination programmes is to eliminate infection. In some cases, however, this is impractical either because the required vaccination coverage cannot be reached, or because the available vaccine is insufficiently effective. In this case, mass vaccination at a level below the herd immunity threshold can disturb the ecological balance of the infection without eliminating it. The consequences of this, as will be seen below, can occasionally be perverse.

Suppose that some proportion q of the population is immunised at birth against an infection with $R_0 > 1$, but that q lies below the critical immunisation threshold. Thus, $q < q_c$. As previously we assume that the population is homogeneously mixing. The effect of this vaccination programme is to change the value of R_0 to R_q, where

$$R_q = R_0 \times (1 - q)$$

This change occurs simply because there are fewer susceptibles to infect. As a result, the average age at infection, A, will also change to a new value A_q in the unvaccinated section of the population, where

$$A_q = \frac{A}{(1-q)}$$

A derivation of this is included in Box 4.2.

Box 4.2 optional | **The post-vaccination average age at infection**

As seen in Chapter 3, in a population with rectangular age structure, we must have

$$R_q = \frac{L}{A_q}$$

The life expectancy, L, is assumed not to be affected by the vaccination programme, an assumption which is reasonable for infections with low mortality. The above equation can be rewritten as

$$A_q = \frac{L}{R_q} = \frac{L}{R_0 \times (1-q)}$$

Since $R_0 = \frac{L}{A}$, it follows that

$$A_q = \frac{L}{\left(\frac{L}{A}\right) \times (1-q)}$$

$$= \frac{A}{(1-q)}$$

○ Suppose that a mumps vaccine is introduced in a population with $A = 7.5$ years and $L = 75$ years, but that only 60% of the population are immunised, i.e. $q = 0.6$. Calculate R_0, q_c, and A_q.

● We have $R_0 = \frac{L}{A} = \frac{75}{7.5} = 10$, and $q_c = 1 - \frac{1}{R_0} = 1 - \frac{1}{10} = 0.9$. The coverage achieved by the vaccination programme is below the critical threshold. The average age at infection in those remaining unimmunised will increase to

$$A_q = \frac{A}{(1-q)} = \frac{7.5}{0.4} = 18.75 \text{ years}$$

Thus the vaccination programme will produce a substantial *increase* in the average age at infection. This makes sense intuitively: immunisation at a level below the critical threshold will not eliminate the infection, but by reducing R_0 it will also reduce the effective contact rate, and hence reduce the force of infection in the unvaccinated population. Hence unvaccinated individuals remain uninfected for longer, and the average age at infection in unvaccinated individuals increases.

This is an example of the impact of *herd immunity*: the unvaccinated individuals experience a reduced force of infection stemming from the presence of a vaccinated subgroup all around them. The vaccinated individuals act as a sort of 'buffer' against infection being transmitted to the unvaccinated.

The fact that vaccination programmes with coverage below the critical immunisation threshold *increase* the average age at infection in the unvaccinated individuals has important implications for vaccination programmes against infections that are more serious at older ages. For example, rubella infection is generally benign in childhood, but rubella infection in pregnancy can cause congenital rubella syndrome (CRS) in the fetus and hence damage the child. In the *absence* of any vaccination programme, most women of child-bearing age will be immune to rubella virus, having been infected by it earlier in life. However, if a *partial* vaccination programme (i.e. with coverage below the critical immunization threshold) is introduced, the average age at infection would increase in those remaining unvaccinated. This could in theory increase susceptibility levels among unvaccinated women of child-bearing age, leading to the perverse result that vaccination, though reducing the *total* number of infections overall, increases the number of infections occurring at older ages, thus causing more cases of CRS than previously arose.

Such **perverse effects** of vaccination programmes below the critical immunisation threshold need careful consideration before the programme is introduced. Epidemic theory is central to the investigation of such effects.

☐ In males, the risk of orchitis (inflammation of the testicles) following mumps infection increases with age. What possible perverse effects of vaccination might you need to consider in these cases? How might you avoid these?

⬤ In theory, low vaccination levels against mumps could increase the total number of cases of orchitis in boys, while reducing the number of mumps infections. The best way to avoid such effects is to keep vaccination levels high; the WHO have suggested that mumps vaccine coverage be kept above 80% to avoid any perverse effects.

Vaccination is not, of course, the only factor affecting the ecology of an infection. For example, in the 1950s, Western countries experienced a large increase in cases of paralytic polio (see Figure 1.4). Paralysis is more likely to result from infection in older age groups. One theory to explain this sudden upsurge was the improvement in hygiene levels in the post-war population. This led, so the theory goes, to a reduction in the value of R_0 for polio virus and hence an increase in the average age at infection, sufficient to result in a big increase in the number of cases of paralytic polio.

☐ Consider another problem. The clinical symptoms of infection with hepatitis A virus increase in severity with age. Suppose that the value of R_0 for hepatitis A virus infection in a given homogeneously mixing population is 4, and that a hepatitis A vaccination programme is to be introduced at birth. Only 50% of the population is likely to get immunised against hepatitis A virus. Calculate the pre- and post-vaccination programme average ages at infection, assuming a rectangular age structure with $L = 75$ years. Discuss the implications of this vaccination programme.

⬤ The pre-vaccination average age at infection is

$$A = \frac{L}{R_0} = \frac{75}{4} = 18.75 \text{ years.}$$

The post-vaccination average age at infection in unvaccinated individuals is

$$A_q = \frac{A}{(1-q)} = \frac{18.75}{1-0.5} = 37.5 \text{ years}$$

The vaccination programme may therefore have negative effects for those remaining unvaccinated: the infection will persist in the population, but unvaccinated people will tend to get infected later, at an age at which the severity of disease is greater.

Vaccination programmes can have other consequences. For example, it has been postulated that if carriage of serogroup C meningitis is largely eradicated by immunisation with meningococcal vaccines specifically targeted against serogroup C meningitis, there is a possibility of expansion of serogroup B meningitis strains into the niche this creates.

In general, vaccination programmes require careful monitoring to check the efficacy of the vaccine, susceptibility levels in the population, and other changes in the epidemiology of the infection including the emergence of new problems due to ecological shifts.

Meningococci are divided into distinct serogroups, according to their polysaccharide outer capsule. The most common serogroups that cause disease worldwide are groups B, C, A, Y and W135. Most disease in the UK is caused by serogroups B and C. Mass vaccination against serogroup C meningitis was introduced in the UK in 1999.

4.3 Eradication and elimination

The ultimate goal of many mass vaccination programmes is the global **eradication** of the infection. Eradication is defined as the reduction of the number of infective organisms to zero: the pathogen is therefore *extinct*. Once an infection is eradicated, the vaccination programme can stop, since there are no more infectious agents. However, to date, only smallpox has been eradicated, though there are increasingly positive signs that the WHO campaign to eradicate polio will also be successful. This theme will be picked up again in the polio case study associated with Book 7.

Eradication is a hugely ambitious goal, because it requires a sustained, concerted effort throughout the globe. While vaccination plays an important part, socio-economic factors and education are also critical in reducing contact rates and transmission risks.

The route to global eradication passes through local **elimination** of the infection. Elimination is defined as the interruption of endemic transmission of infection. This occurs if each infectious individual in the population infects on average less than one other. Elimination is achieved locally by maintaining immunisation levels above the critical immunisation threshold q.

Unlike eradication, elimination can be achieved locally, within the framework of national vaccination programmes. For example, measles infection has been eliminated in much of the American continent, thanks to mass vaccination.

Eradication and elimination are often confused, but are conceptually quite different. For example, elimination requires the maintenance of high levels of vaccination, but it does not imply that infections do not occur. These will inevitably arise through imported cases from other countries. However, such importations cannot lead to the re-establishment of endemic transmission of infection in a population with an effective vaccination programme.

It is important, nevertheless, to remember that vaccination is only one among many control strategies. As yet there are no effective vaccines against many infectious agents, for example, HIV, malaria, leishmanias, haemorrhagic viruses. Thus, many deaths from infectious diseases worldwide are not vaccine-preventable.

4.4 Revisiting the assumptions

The results of this and previous chapters were derived under a number of assumptions. In the present section we briefly discuss the effect of relaxing some of these assumptions.

The main assumption was that the population is homogeneously mixing. This is clearly an oversimplification: in most circumstances mixing is heterogeneous. In particular, contact rates vary with age, so that the force of infection is age-dependent. Age-dependent forces of infection can be estimated from serological survey data and case notifications, using an extension of the methods described in Section 3.3. An example of age-dependent forces of infection for mumps and rubella in the UK, derived from serological data, is shown in Figure 4.1.

Other heterogeneities include individual variation in contact rates, which are particularly important for sexually transmitted infections, and variations due to small-scale social structures, such as family or school contacts.

All these heterogeneities may be accommodated in more general definitions of the basic reproduction number, R_0, and the critical immunisation threshold q_c, which are beyond the scope of this book. However, the interpretation of these parameters remains the same as under homogeneous mixing. Nevertheless, estimating them is much more difficult, and is an active topic of research.

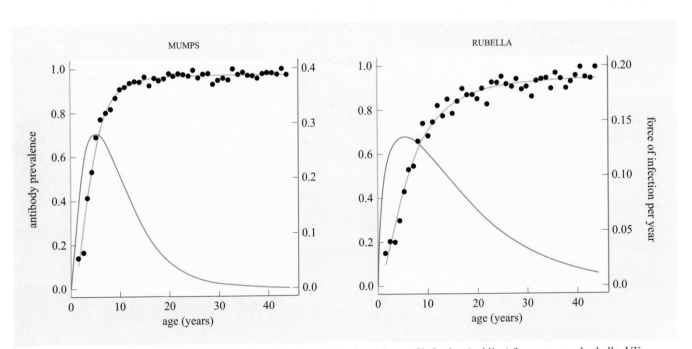

FIGURE 4.1 Serological survey data (dots, with blue line through them) and force of infection (red line) for mumps and rubella, UK 1986–7. The rubella data are for boys only. For both infections the force of infection is highly peaked in childhood, reflecting increased contact rates in school-age children.

In Chapter 4 we considered infections in an endemic steady state. This led to the relationship

$$R_0 = \frac{1}{S}$$

where S is the proportion susceptible. This fundamental relationship may also be generalised to heterogeneously mixing populations, though at the cost of greater mathematical complexity.

These concepts can also be applied to infections transmitted *indirectly*. Indeed, the threshold phenomenon in infectious diseases was first appreciated for malaria by Sir Ronald Ross, early in the twentieth century. Ross discovered that the mosquito density had to be above a certain threshold for malaria to be maintained in an endemic state. Inevitably, vector-borne infections are more complex than those directly transmitted, as the biology and ecology of the vector and its interaction with human hosts must be taken into account. Thus, for malaria, dengue and yellow fever, all of which are transmitted via mosquitoes, mosquito density and biting rates enter into the definition of R_0. The concept of R_0 also plays a role in macroparasitic diseases, though again with additional complications: for example, the worm burden (the number of worms carried by a case) and its distribution is important for worm infestations.

The concepts of elimination and eradication also apply to macroparasitic and vector-borne infections. For vector-borne infections, interventions aimed at the vectors may also be important, as with the use of bed nets and insecticide against mosquitoes in malaria control.

Summary of Chapter 4

1   The basic reproduction number is related to the critical immunisation threshold, which is the minimum proportion of the population that must be immunised to eliminate the infection.

2   Vaccination at levels under the critical immunisation threshold alters the ecology of the infection, and can have perverse effects.

3   Mass vaccination programmes can seek elimination or eradication of an infection. Elimination is the interruption of sustained transmission of an infection; eradication is the reduction of the number of infections to zero.

5 DYNAMICS OF INFECTION

In Chapters 3 and 4 we dealt primarily with infections in endemic steady state. This state is characterized by regular fluctuations around a long-term average. In Chapter 4 we used this average endemic level to derive simple expressions for key epidemiological parameters, which can be estimated from surveillance data. In the present chapter, we focus attention on the *fluctuations* around the long-term average level.

5.1 Epidemicity

A striking feature of many infectious diseases, particularly the common infections of childhood, is that they come in regular epidemic waves, often spaced out by a period of several years. This phenomenon is known as **epidemicity**. The interval between successive epidemics is called the **inter-epidemic period**, or epidemic period for short, and will be denoted T. The regularity of these epidemics is remarkable. For instance, prior to the introduction of measles vaccine in 1968, epidemics of measles occurred in the UK every two years, as shown by the graph of notified cases in Figure 5.1.

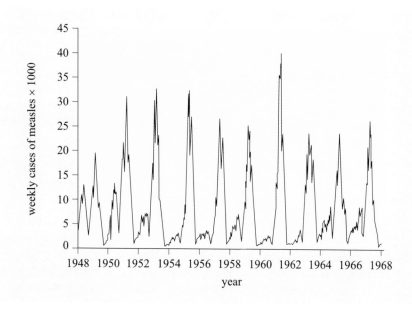

FIGURE 5.1 Measles notifications, England and Wales, 1948–68, prior to the introduction of measles vaccination.

Similar epidemic cycles can be observed for other infections: Figure 5.2, for example, shows a time series of whooping cough notifications in the UK.

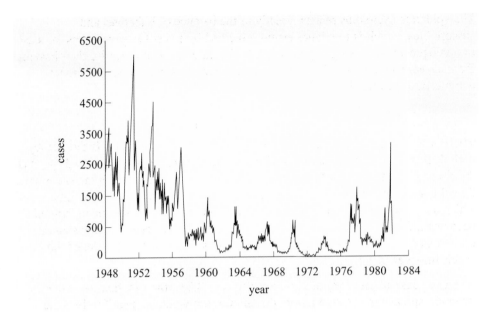

FIGURE 5.2
Whooping cough notifications, England and Wales, 1948–1982. Pertussis vaccination was introduced in the 1950s.

○ Use Figure 5.2 to estimate (roughly) the epidemic period for whooping cough in the UK.

● The epidemic period is about 3–4 years.

Both measles and whooping cough display annual as well as longer epidemic cycles (these annual cycles are reasonably clear for measles in Figure 5.1, rather less clear for whooping cough in Figure 5.2). It is important to distinguish between the two types of cycles, as they are due to different mechanisms.

Regular annual cycles in incidence may be due to changes in the contact rate or transmission risk which vary seasonally. For example, the incidence of measles has been shown to peak during school terms, and to decrease during school holidays. This is a clear indication that transmission between children at school plays a key role in the epidemiology of measles.

However, such seasonal effects cannot explain the occurrence of epidemic cycles occurring at intervals of more than one year. To understand why, and when, such cycles occur, it is necessary to return to the SIR model of Chapter 2.

Suppose that an infectious individual were introduced into a large susceptible population, in which $R_0 > 1$. Clearly, the number of infected individuals $I(t)$ will grow initially as the infection spreads through the population. At the same time, provided of course that the infection confers immunity, the number of susceptibles $S(t)$ will drop as more are infected. Eventually, the number of susceptibles will drop to such an extent that most of the contacts made by an infectious individual are with immunes, and hence do not result in new infections. Eventually, the number of new infections will drop. At this point two scenarios can develop. If the number of new infections falls rapidly compared to the birth rate, $I(t)$ may eventually drop to zero. This is the phenomenon of stochastic extinction (see Box 3.1). However, if the birth rate is high enough, then the susceptibles $S(t)$ will be replenished sufficiently rapidly to stem the drop in $I(t)$ before it reaches zero. Thus the incidence of infection will bottom out and begin increasing again. This is the pattern observed for infections like measles and whooping cough in the UK, prior to the introduction of vaccination.

The epidemic cycle thus relates directly to the balance of infectives and susceptibles, which is to a large extent governed by a few key parameters (at least in homogeneously mixing populations). It should come as no surprise therefore that the inter-epidemic period T is related, at least approximately, to some of these parameters. Specifically,

$$T \approx 2\pi\sqrt{A \times (D' + D)}$$

where A is the average age at infection, D' (pronounced 'dee-dash') is the latency period, D is the infectious period, and π (the Greek symbol pi, pronounced 'pie') is the constant 3.1417... . Note that A, D' and D must be expressed in the same units. Recall that the latency period of an infection is the period between the point at which an individual becomes infected and the time at which that same individual becomes infectious. Therefore, the sum $D' + D$ is the average time between an individual becoming infected and infecting others; this is sometimes called the **serial interval** of the infection.

To make sense of this relationship (see also Box 3.2), note first that the faster the infection spreads in the population, the shorter you would expect T to be. One factor affecting the speed at which infection spreads is the force of infection: the more people are infected per unit time, the faster the spread. Thus infection spreads more rapidly if the force of infection λ is high, and hence if the average age at infection A is low (since $A = 1/\lambda$). Thus T should decrease as A decreases. This is what the formula for T implies: as T and A are on opposite sides of the equation, so a decrease in A has a similar effect on T. Another factor affecting the speed of spread is the serial interval $D' + D$: the shorter the time between successive generations, the quicker the spread will be. Thus T should decrease as $D' + D$ decreases. Again, this is what the formula for T implies. Finally, do not worry about the other aspects of the equation, such as the square root or the number 2π in the equation (2π is there because this is a cyclic process – if you have studied geometry, you will recall that the number π is bound up with the geometry of the circle). The key thing is to check that the equation makes sense to you from a qualitative point of view.

Note finally that the equation is an approximation, which breaks down as the infectious period increases: infections with long infectious periods tend not to display regular epidemic cycles.

Table 5.1 gives values for A, D' and D for some common infections of childhood in developed countries.

Table 5.1 Typical values of A, D' and D for selected infections in developed countries. These values are indicative: A varies between populations, and D' and D vary between individuals.

Infection	A (years)	D' (days)	D (days)
measles	5	5	5
mumps	5	8	12
rubella	8	10	12
varicella zoster	7	10	8
pertussis	5	6	15

For measles in the UK, $D' + D = 10$ days $= 10/365 \approx 0.027$ years. Prior to mass vaccination, the average age at infection was about 5 years. Hence

$$T \approx 2 \times 3.142 \times \sqrt{5 \times 0.027} \approx 2.3 \text{ years}$$

This accords reasonably well with the observed inter-epidemic period of 2 years.

○ Use data from Table 5.1 to calculate the epidemic period of whooping cough. Does this calculation match the observed cycle in Figure 5.2?

● $T \approx 2 \times 3.142 \times \sqrt{5 \times (21/365)} \approx 3.4 \text{ years}$

The observed epidemic period varies between 3 and 4 years, so again theory is in agreement with observation.

The introduction of mass vaccination can have a direct impact on the epidemic cycle. Since vaccination increases the average age at infection, the epidemic period T will lengthen, and regular epidemics might even disappear entirely.

5.2 A final note on modelling epidemics

Epidemic models have become an essential tool of epidemiologists, and are commonly used to investigate the ways in which an infection spreads through a population, and to explore the consequences of vaccination strategies.

Many epidemic models are based on the compartmental SIR model (see Section 2.2). Simple mathematical equations can be used to describe the progress of an infection through a population. These models, known as *deterministic* models, successfully replicate most of the features of infectious diseases. One feature they cannot replicate, however, is sustained epidemic cycles: the oscillations of deterministic models eventually settle down to an equilibrium level, as shown for example in Figure 5.3.

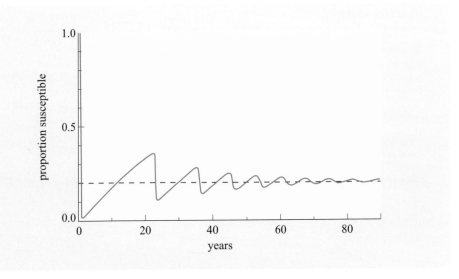

FIGURE 5.3 Proportion susceptible over time as predicted by a deterministic model. The model produces epidemic fluctuations, but these eventually settle down to an equilibrium level (dotted line), a phenomenon not observed in real life.

Another feature not reproduced by deterministic models is stochastic extinction (Box 3.1). More generally, when the number of cases is small, it is necessary to allow for random fluctuations. More complex models, known as *stochastic* models, have been developed to take account of such random effects.

Summary of Chapter 5

1   Endemic infections with short latency and infectious periods often exhibit regular epidemic cycles. These cycles are related to the build up of susceptibles through births, and their depletion by infections that result in immunity.

2   For infections exhibiting epidemicity, the inter-epidemic period is related to the average age at infection and the serial interval of the infection.

3   Epidemic models offer insights on population effects on the spread of infectious agents which are essential in designing effective control strategies.

CONCLUDING REMARKS

Throughout Book 6, the emphasis has been on understanding the dynamics of how infections spread through populations, how they can become established, and how they might be eliminated or eradicated by vaccination. In spite of their shortcomings, epidemic models are central to our understanding of infectious diseases. At a conceptual level, these models help focus attention on important threshold effects, such as the qualitative difference between the spread of infections with $R_0 < 1$ compared to those with $R_0 > 1$, or the role played by the herd immunity level and critical immunisation threshold for endemic infections. At a more practical level, the quantitative insights offered by epidemic models are essential in designing effective control strategies. The key message from Book 6 is that the control of infectious diseases requires a population and social perspective on the spread of infectious agents, as well as an understanding of the biology of the pathogens and their impact on individuals.

LEARNING OUTCOMES

When you have studied Book 6, you should be able to:

6.1 Define and use, or recognise definitions and applications of, each of the terms printed in **bold** in the text. (*Questions 6.1–6.8*)

6.2 Calculate risks and rates in simple settings. (*Question 6.1*)

6.3 Describe and contrast the types of data and surveillance systems commonly available for infectious diseases. (*Question 6.8*)

6.4 Interpret data on case reports and serological surveys of infectious diseases. (*Questions 6.1–6.4 and 6.6*)

6.5 Interpret schematic representations of simple compartmental models such as the SIR model. (*Question 6.7*)

6.6 Estimate and interpret the reproduction number for infections in susceptible populations from outbreak data. (*Question 6.2*)

6.7 Estimate and interpret the reproduction number R_0 and critical immunisation threshold q_c, given information on the herd immunity level or the average age at infection in homogeneously mixing populations in an endemic steady state. (*Questions 6.3 and 6.4*)

6.8 Discuss, with examples, the impact of mass vaccination programmes and possible perverse effects. (*Questions 6.5 and 6.6*)

6.9 Contrast strategies of elimination and eradication for mass vaccination programmes. (*Questions 6.3 and 6.4*)

6.10 Describe and interpret the phenomenon of epidemicity for endemic infections. (*Question 6.6*)

QUESTIONS FOR BOOK 6

Question 6.1

A hepatitis A virus outbreak occurs in a school of 100 children, all of whom may be assumed to be susceptible. A total of 20 children became jaundiced (a common symptom of this infection).

(a) Calculate the risk of hepatitis A virus infection for these children.

(b) Hepatitis A infection in children is often asymptomatic. How might this affect your risk estimate? What further analyses might you undertake?

Question 6.2

Monkeypox is a zoonotic infection caused by an orthopox virus believed to circulate among squirrels in central Africa. The virus can be transmitted to humans and causes a disease similar to smallpox. In 1980–84, 209 human monkeypox cases were reported from rural areas of Zaire. Of these 209 cases, 147 are thought to have been infected by contact with animals. These 147 cases directly infected 47 others.

(a) Calculate an estimate of the basic reproduction number R_0 for human monkeypox in rural Zaire.

(b) Discuss the potential for human monkeypox to become endemic in this population. What may happen if the infection were to spread to more densely populated areas?

(c) Smallpox vaccine also protects against monkeypox. Smallpox vaccination ceased in the late 1970s. In 1996, another outbreak of monkeypox occurred in rural Zaire, with a higher attack rate among adults than occurred in 1980–84. Discuss the implications of these observations for the estimate of R_0 which you obtained in part (a).

Question 6.3

Parvovirus B19 causes a rash-like illness called Fifth disease. In a serological survey in the UK, the following proportions were found to have antibody to parvovirus (presence of antibody indicates immunity):

Age group (years)	Proportion with antibody
0–5	0.171
6–10	0.373
11–20	0.543
21–30	0.537
31+	0.604

(a) (Optional) Assuming a rectangular age distribution (everyone dying on their 75th birthday), show that the overall proportion susceptible to parvovirus in this population is 0.463.

(b) Given that the proportion susceptible to parvovirus B19 is 0.463, obtain an estimate of the basic reproduction number, R_0. What assumptions have you made?

(c) What proportion of the population would have to be vaccinated if parvovirus B19 were to be eliminated from this population? What other steps would be required to eradicate parvovirus B19?

Question 6.4

The following data on measles are part of a famous dataset assembled by Dr Hope-Simpson in Cirencester, England, between 1947 and 1950.

Age group (years)	Observed cases
<1	10
1	33
2	28
3	28
4	46
5	53
6	39
7	37
8	18
9	10

(a) (Optional) Calculate the average age at infection, assuming that no cases of measles occurred after age 10. (In the 1940s, few cases occurred after this age.)

(b) The average age at infection in this population is 5 years. Hence calculate the basic reproduction number R_0 and the critical immunisation threshold q_c for measles, assuming that the population is homogeneously mixing with rectangular age structure and $L = 70$ years.

(c) Can measles be eliminated in this population, with a vaccine that confers immunity in 95% of those vaccinated?

Question 6.5

Prior to the introduction in the UK of universal rubella vaccination at 15 months as part of the MMR vaccination programme, girls aged 10–14 years were vaccinated and boys were not vaccinated against rubella. Discuss the logic behind these two approaches to the control of rubella, and identify arguments for and against each approach.

Question 6.6

Figure 5.2 shows the graph of notified cases of whooping cough in England and Wales, 1948–1982. Pertussis vaccination was introduced in the 1950s. Vaccine coverage was high, exceeding 80% in the early 1970s. In 1974, public concern about the safety of the vaccine led to a precipitous decline in vaccine coverage, to little over 30% a few years later. Thereafter, confidence in the vaccine gradually returned and vaccine coverage increased again.

(a) Discuss the trends in notifications in Figure 5.2 in the light of these facts about the vaccine.

(b) It is sometimes claimed (for example, by some groups opposed to vaccination) that vaccination played only a minor role in the control of infections, which is primarily attributable to general improvements in health. Discuss this proposition in the light of these data.

(c) According to epidemic theory, high vaccination levels should increase the average age at infection and hence the inter-epidemic period. Contrast this theoretical effect of vaccination with the observed effect on the epidemic period of whooping cough as shown in Figure 5.2. Can you suggest an explanation that reconciles the difference between theory and observation?

Question 6.7

The SIRS model extends the SIR model in that individuals in the recovered compartment R may lose immunity and revert to the susceptible compartment S. This model might be appropriate to represent infection with *Vibrio cholerae* bacteria, transmitted by the faecal-oral route (primarily by ingestion of contaminated water) or direct contact. Draw a diagram to represent the SIRS model as a compartmental model.

Question 6.8

It is required to set up a surveillance system to obtain information on the incidence of an uncommon infection primarily affecting young children. The main symptom of this infection is a measles-like rash. Contrast the relative merits of using (a) the statutory notification system, (b) an active surveillance system based on paediatricians, (c) laboratory reports to obtain the information required. What surveillance system or combination of surveillance systems would you recommend?

ANSWERS TO QUESTIONS

QUESTION 6.1

(a) The risk is $20/100 = 0.2$.

(b) Jaundice is a clinical manifestation of hepatitis A. Since many infections are likely to be asymptomatic, it is probable that the risk estimate is too low. Further analyses could include testing of blood samples for antibodies to hepatitis A virus.

QUESTION 6.2

(a) An estimate of R_0 is $47/147 \approx 0.32$.

(b) Since R_0 is less than 1, human monkeypox cannot become endemic in this rural population. However, if the infection were to spread to a population with higher contact rates, as might occur in a more densely populated area, then R_0 would rise. If it increased above 1 then the infection could become endemic in humans.

(c) The higher attack rate in adults in the 1996–97 outbreak may be the result of higher susceptibility in this age group, following the ending of smallpox vaccination. The value of R_0 calculated in (a) should be revised upwards to take account of this change in susceptibility levels.

QUESTION 6.3

(a) You may have noticed that the proportion with antibody is slightly higher in the 11–20-year-olds than in the 21–30-year-olds. This is most probably due to random variation. First, obtain the proportions susceptible in each age group, and the proportion of the population within each age group under the rectangular assumption (everyone lives exactly 75 years). These are given in the following table:

Age group (completed years)	Proportion susceptible	Proportion of population
0–5	0.829	6/75
6–10	0.627	5/75
11–20	0.457	10/75
21–30	0.463	10/75
31–74	0.396	44/75

The proportion susceptible is then

$$S = 0.829 \times \frac{6}{75} + 0.627 \times \frac{5}{75} + 0.457 \times \frac{10}{75} + 0.463 \times \frac{10}{75} + 0.396 \times \frac{44}{75}$$
$$\approx 0.463$$

(b) Assuming that parvovirus B19 is in an endemic steady state, and that the populations is homogeneously mixing, an estimate of the basic reproduction number is:

$$R_0 = \frac{1}{S} = \frac{1}{0.463} \approx 2.2$$

(c) The critical immunisation threshold is

$$q_c = 1 - S - 0.463 = 0.537$$

Thus about 54% of this population would have to be vaccinated to eliminate parvovirus B19 infection. However, the infection would not be eradicated unless parvovirus B19 infection were eliminated throughout the world.

QUESTION 6.4

(a) The total number of cases is 302. Using the age group midpoints (0.5, 1.5, ..., 9.5), the average age at infection is

$$A = \frac{(0.5 \times 10 + 1.5 \times 33 + 2.5 \times 28 + 3.5 \times 28 + 4.5 \times 46 + 5.5 \times 53 + 6.5 \times 39 + 7.5 \times 37 + 8.5 \times 18 + 9.5 \times 10)}{302}$$

$$\approx 5.0 \text{ years}$$

(b) The basic reproduction number is

$$R_0 = \frac{L}{A} = \frac{70}{5} = 14$$

and the critical immunisation threshold is

$$q_c = 1 - \frac{1}{R_0} = 1 - \frac{1}{14} \approx 0.93$$

(c) Yes – just. If 100% of the population are vaccinated with this vaccine, then 95% will be immune. This is above the critical immunisation threshold, so measles will not persist in this population.

QUESTION 6.5

The logic of the selective vaccination programme for girls is to ensure that women of child-bearing age are protected against rubella, and hence that any children they may have are not at risk of congenital rubella syndrome (CRS). This vaccination programme does not aim at elimination (or eradication) of rubella, since boys are not vaccinated and rubella virus still circulates in the population. The advantage of this strategy is that it targets directly the group most at risk, i.e. women, in whom high vaccine coverage can therefore be achieved. Its disadvantage is that the force of rubella infection in unvaccinated women (or in vaccinated women in whom the vaccine is ineffective) will still be high, due to continuing circulation of the virus amongst males and unvaccinated females.

The logic of the universal vaccination programme is to protect women from rubella, but also to reduce the force of infection in those women who remain susceptible. The advantage of this strategy is that, if vaccine coverage is sufficiently high that the proportion immunised exceeds the critical threshold, then rubella infection will be eliminated and both vaccinated and unvaccinated women will be protected. The disadvantage is that if high vaccine coverage is not achieved in the population as a whole, the average age at infection will increase, possibly resulting in an increase in CRS cases.

QUESTION 6.6

(a) It is possible to distinguish three phases in Figure 5.2. Phase 1 lasts until the late 1950s, and is characterised by high but declining incidence of whooping cough. This corresponds to the pre-vaccination era. The decline over this period could be due to general improvements in health, treatment due to antibiotics (and hence reduced propensity to notify cases, perceived as less serious), and gradual introduction of vaccination. Phase 2 lasts from 1960 to 1976, and corresponds to the high vaccine coverage period prior to the crisis over whooping cough vaccine safety. This phase is characterised by a marked reduction in incidence, though regular epidemics persist. Phase 3 is the period of reduced vaccine uptake from 1976 to 1982, accompanied by an upsurge in notifications to levels not seen since the introduction of mass vaccination. (Since the early 1980s, vaccine uptake increased to reach current levels of about 90%, while whooping cough incidence declined).

(b) The decline in notifications in the 1950s, prior to mass vaccination, lends support to the argument that general improvements in health, nutrition and social conditions have played a role in the control of infectious diseases. However the upsurge in cases after the collapse in vaccine coverage in the mid-1970s shows that vaccination also plays a key role in controlling infection.

(c) The inter-epidemic period for whooping cough appears to have remained roughly constant throughout the period 1948–1982, irrespective of the level of vaccination coverage. It has been suggested that vaccination reduces the severity of symptoms, but does not protect (or protect completely) against infection. If this were the case, vaccination would not affect (or only affect marginally) the inter-epidemic period.

QUESTION 6.7

The SIRS model may be represented by Figure 6.7.

QUESTION 6.8

(a) Using the statutory notification system is not a good idea, since the infection is uncommon, and produces a measles-like rash which would probably be mistaken for measles. Thus case reports are likely to be very inaccurate. (b) An active surveillance system based on paediatricians might be better focused, since the infection occurs mainly in young children. However, the non-specificity of the symptoms would still be a problem. (c) Laboratory reports would solve the problem of non-specificity of clinical diagnoses, but incidence rates might be underestimated as most doctors would not seek laboratory confirmation of the infectious agent in rash-like diseases. The best combination might be a sentinel active surveillance system based on selected paediatricians, supplemented by laboratory confirmation of clinical cases.

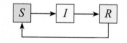

FIGURE 6.7
The SIRS model represented as a compartmental model.

FURTHER SOURCES

Current and past data on infectious diseases may be obtained from the organisations listed on the *Resources* section of the course website; further information can be obtained by navigating to the links available from these sites.

ACKNOWLEDGMENTS

Grateful acknowledgement is made to the following sources for permission to reproduce material in this book:

Cover

Colour transmission electron micrograph of a section through a mumps virus in a capsule. M. Aymard, ISM/Science Photo Library.

Figures

Figure 1.1: Reprinted with permission from p. 103 of F. R. Moulton (1947), *Aerobiology*, Washington DC, American Association for the Advancement of Science; *Figure 1.2*: Gustafson, T. L., Lievens, A. W. *et al*. 'Measles outbreak in a fully immunized secondary-school population' *The New England Journal of Medicine*, Vol. 316, No. 13 (1987) Massachusetts Medical Society; *Figures 1.4, 2.1, 1.9b, 3.1, 5.1, 5.2* and *5.3*: Anderson, R. M. and May, R. M. (1991) *Infectious Diseases of Humans; Dynamics and Control*, reprinted by permission of Oxford University Press; *Figure 1.5*: Farrington, C. P., Andrews, N. J., Beale, A. D. and Catchpole, M. A. (1996) *Journal of the Royal Statistical Society, Series A (Statistics in Society)*, Vol. 159, Issue 3, pp. 547–563, © Royal Statistical Society; *Figure 2.6*: Brisson, M. *et al*. (2001) 'Epidemiology of varicella zoster virus infection in Canada and the United Kingdom, *Epidemiology and Infection*, **127**, pp. 305–314, Figure 1(b), Cambridge University Press; *Figure 2.7*: Reprinted with permission from p. 102 of Moulton F. R. (1947), *Aerobiology*, American Association for the Advancement of Science, Washington DC; *Figure 2.9a*: Nokes, D. J., Anderson, R. M. and Anderson, M. J. (1986) 'Rubella epidemiology in South East England', *Journal of Hygiene*, **86**, pp. 291–304, Cambridge University Press; *Figure 3.2*: Reseau Sentinelles, http://www.b3e.jussieu.fr/sentiweb; *Figure 4.1*: Farrington, C. P., Kanaan, M. N. and Gay, N. J. (2001) 'Estimation of the basic reproduction number for infectious diseases from age-stratified serological survey data', *Applied Statistics*, **50**, Part 3, pp. 251–292, © Royal Statistical Society; *Figure 6.4*: Griffiths, D. A. (1974) 'A catalytic model of infection for measles', *Applied Statistics*, **23**, No. 3, p. 330, © Royal Statistical Society.

Every effort has been made to trace all the copyright owners, but if any has been inadvertently overlooked, the publishers will be pleased to make the necessary arrangements at the first opportunity.

INDEX

Note: Entries in **bold** are key terms. Page numbers referring to information that is given only in a figure or caption are printed in *italics*.